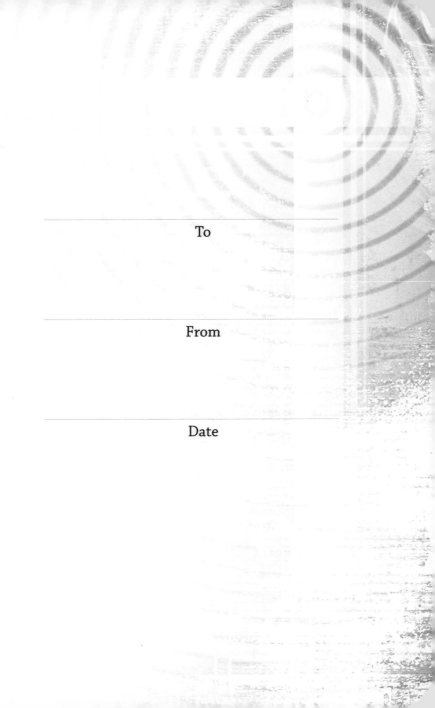

To

From

Date

ONE DAY BETTER
A SPORTS DEVOTIONAL

by Jere Johnson

summerside
PRESS

One Day Better (Guys) © 2009 by Jere Johnson

ISBN 978-1-935416-14-2

Special thanks to FCA's *Sharing the Victory* magazine (www.sharingthevictory.com) for use of their material and to these athletic teams for permission to reprint: The San Diego Chargers/LaDainian Tomlinson; The University of Washington/Lorenzo Romar; St. Louis Cardinals/Albert Pujols. Thanks also to Derwin Gray, Jason Wright, Mark Cahill, and Drew Neitzel for their involvement with this project and the photos provided. Photo credits: Derwin Gray courtesy of Ralf Melvin Photography, http://www.ralphmelvin.com; LaDainian Tomlinson courtesy of Mike Nowak/San Diego Chargers; Albert Pujols courtesy of Scott Rovak/St. Louis Cardinals; Lorenzo Romar courtesy of Cliff DesPeaux; Drew Neitzel courtesy of Rolf Kamper; Mark Cahill used by permission (markcahill.org).

Scripture quotations marked HCSB have been taken from the Holman Christian Standard Bible © copyright 2000 by Holman Bible Publishers. Used by permission. Scripture quotations marked NLT are taken from the *Holy Bible*, New Living Translation, copyright © 1996. Used by permission of Tyndale House Publishers, Inc. Wheaton, Illinois 60189, U.S.A. All rights reserved. Scripture quotations marked NIV are taken from the Holy Bible, New International Version®. NIV®. Copyright © 1973, 1978, 1984 by International Bible Society. Used by permission of Zondervan. All rights reserved. Scripture quotations marked ESV are taken from The Holy Bible, English Standard Version®, copyright © 2001 by Crossway Bibles, a publishing ministry of Good News Publishers. Used by permission. All rights reserved. Scripture quotations marked KJV are taken from the King James Version of the Bible. Scripture quotations marked CEV are from the Contemporary English Version, Copyright © 1991, 1992, 1995 by American Bible Society. Used by permission.

Cover and interior design by Kirk DouPonce of DogEared Design | www.DogEaredDesign.com. Typesetting by James Baker of James Baker Design | www.jamesbakerdesign.com.

Published by Summerside Press, Inc., 11024 Quebec Circle, Bloomington, Minnesota 55438 | www.summersidepress.com

Summerside Press™ is an inspirational publisher offering fresh, irresistible books to uplift the heart and delight the mind.

Printed in China.

I would like to dedicate this book to the following people:

My Lord and Savior Jesus Christ...
for without Him nothing would be possible for me.
1 Corinthians 10:31

My beautiful wife, Stacey...
who has inspired me to be a better husband, father, and friend.

My wonderful children Lauren, Caleb, and Evan...
you give me the joy of being your dad each day.

My parents, Jim and Carolyn Johnson...
who taught me to believe in myself no matter what happens in life.

My mentors, Chuck Mealy and Aidan McKenzie...
who have encouraged me to be all I can be for Christ and to serve others first.

Finally, my son, Luke Robert Johnson...
who during his short life inspired me to write, to love, to learn, and to lean
on the One who gives and takes away. Luke, I write today because of you.
Enjoy heaven until we meet again someday.

CONTENTS

FOREWORD
BY DAN BRITTON

Time usually does one of two things—bring you closer to God or draw you further away from God. One thing is for sure. You never just stay the same. Each day, you choose to move into a growing relationship with Jesus or move away from the Lord.

The book you are holding in your hands will challenge you to dig deep. *One Day Better* by Jere Johnson is a book that will help move you into a passionate relationship with Jesus. If you just want to be the same old athlete, then I encourage you to give this book to someone who wants to grow and learn. Each sports devotion will develop your spiritual foundation so that Christ will take you to a deeper level. Also, the "Get Real with God" stories will inspire you as professional athletes, top college players, and coaches share their spiritual insights.

The Lord wants to work in your life in a powerful way through this devotional book. He will shape, mold, and form you to be a true woman of God. God wants to give you boldness in your spirit to love God without limits or hesitations. Your spiritual confidence in Christ is much more important than your athletic confidence. You will be motivated to let the Holy Spirit control the very core of your life, from the inside out!

I have personally been reading Jere's devotions for years. His devotions have trained me spiritually and pushed me to love God. Being an athlete, you know a good workout produces a ton of sweat. I love to sweat because it means that I am accomplishing something. In 1 Timothy 4:7–8, Paul writes "Train yourself to be godly. For physical training is of some value, but godliness has value for all things" (NIV). The word *train* in Greek means to exercise or work out. God desires us to have "spiritual sweat"—training for godliness. "Spiritual sweat" comes when we get alone with our Savior and spend intimate, deep, rich time in the Word. He works us out—dealing with sin and revealing areas that need to be changed in our life. This only comes during our times with our Lord. *One Day Better* will produce spiritual sweat in your life.

Get plugged in and start reading *One Day Better* today. It will be your decision to move toward God. It might be one of the most important decisions you make.

Dan Britton
Sr. Vice President of Ministry Advancement
Fellowship of Christian Athletes

INTRODUCTION

As I grew up in Indiana, basketball was always part of my life. When I got a new basketball, I would play with it until it was smooth and about ready to pop. I worked hard to become a better player. I was fortunate to play three years of varsity high school basketball and learned many valuable lessons which have carried me throughout life.

The love of basketball took me into over twenty years of coaching, but in 1999, my life as a coach was turned upside down. My third child, Luke, was born with many special needs and required close to three months in the hospital before he could come home. Luke struggled with health conditions for his entire life of two years before God called him home. I learned during his life what it meant to be one day better. Every day that we went to the hospital to see him, we wanted to see progress. We wanted to see improvement. We wanted to see him getting better each day. He did get better, but in December 2001, Luke went to be with the Lord. His life is now better than ever, and he finally gets to run the streets of gold. The Lord gave me the gift of writing during Luke's life and now has given me the opportunity to start my own sports devotional site at www.sportsdevo.com.

As I continue to work with student athletes through the Fellowship of Christian Athletes or the youth sports that I coach, I strive to use the same One Day Better principle in their athletic lives. Too many athletes today do not put in the effort it takes to achieve the goals in their sport. They want the end results without all the work it takes to get there. I challenge my athletes with the question, "What are you going to do today to be better than yesterday?" They have to think and be prepared to respond immediately. The response I hear is always interesting, but it gives them a goal to strive for that day and beyond.

Having the opportunity to serve the Lord through FCA, my challenge to student athletes and coaches is to use the One Day Better principle in their spiritual walk, as well. We need to strive to grow in Christ each day through reading His Word, prayer, and fellowship with others who will encourage us in our walk with Christ.

As you read through this devotional book, I pray that it will help you draw closer to Christ. You will be inspired by the "Get Real with God" sections. Take the next thirty days to read through this book, write down your thoughts and prayers, and decide for yourself to become "One Day Better" as an athlete, friend, and one who wants to grow in Christ. May this book be a blessing to your life as you strive to live for Him!

Expect great things from God,
attempt great things for God.

William Carey

Laced Up

"Protect me, LORD, from the clutches of the wicked. Keep me safe from violent men who plan to make me stumble" (Psalm 140:4 HCSB).

SET:

Fred was a very good player in my high school program. He could run, jump, dunk, and shoot. He had all the tools he needed in order to be successful, but Fred made a big mistake one day. He came out to practice late, and I did not see him until "it" happened. We were doing our warm-up layup drill when Fred came down after a layup and turned his ankle badly. When I looked at his feet, I realized that he was not prepared for the drill. Fred's shoes were untied and not laced up tight for practice. He tripped over his laces, tore up his ankle, and missed the remainder of our season.

Are you properly "laced up" spiritually? What does that mean? When we become spiritually relaxed and do not make sure we are ready to compete against Satan and his schemes, it is easy to be tripped up by the world and all it offers. Let's take a look at how the world wants to trip us up....

Look at slogans today. Burger King: "Have it *your* way." The army: "Be all *you* can be." Sprite: "Obey *your* thirst." And it goes on and on. These slogans and products themselves are not bad, but the world tells us that we can do it on our own and that *you* are all you need. Jesus Christ offers us a different way. He wants us to be laced up in Him, ready in

Him—in His Word and laced up spiritually—so that we are ready to battle the enemy.

I don't know if Fred would have turned his ankle that day or not if his shoes had been tied properly. But I do know that if they had been properly laced, an untied shoe wouldn't have caused his injury. In your life with Christ, are you leaving your spiritual shoes untied and hoping not to be tripped up by the evil one? Take time each day to make sure you are ready to compete for Christ. Spend time in prayer and in His Word, and focus on Him throughout the day. Do this and I know you will be less likely to be tripped up.

Before you go out into the world today, ask yourself if you are ready to compete against what it offers. If not, get laced up in Christ right now! You won't regret it!

GO:

1. How often do you get tripped up by what the world offers?

2. Do you make sure you are "laced up" in Christ every day?

3. Today, how can you start to be more laced up in Christ?

WORKOUT:

Job 18:7
Psalm 36:11; 37:24; 119:165
Ephesians 6:10–18

True Power

"I love God's law with all my heart. But there is another power within me that is at war with my mind. This power makes me a slave to the sin that is still within me" (Romans 7:22–23 NLT).

I love watching football. I love watching those 300-pound linemen push their opponents down the field. Their discipline in holding their block for ten, fifteen, or more yards is always impressive. The power they show and keep throughout a play separates the good from the great.

I have known many players like this over the years who had the power to drive their opponents into the ground but did not have discipline or power when it came to other areas of life. They couldn't help but click a mouse and go to Internet sites they didn't need to go to. They didn't have the ability to say no to others who wanted them to drink, do drugs, or engage in sexual activities. They left their discipline on the field.

Paul speaks of this battle in Romans 7. Though Paul loves God's Word, there is a power within him—and each of us—that is at war with the mind. What is this thing so powerful that it causes us to struggle and wrestle in this way? It is our sinful nature and desires. And I am as guilty as the next person. As an athlete, I was disciplined to follow through on the given play, game plan, or strategy, but off the field I did not always practice the same discipline.

True power is tapping into the only Source that

can give us the proper desires and discipline to make necessary changes so that we can do the right things. That power only comes from a personal relationship with Jesus Christ and by spending time with and growing in Him. Christ will give us the power to stay away from the things that cause us to battle internally.

If you have the discipline to follow through on your game plan for your team, surely, with God's power, you have the discipline to follow His plan for your life. Continue to be plugged in to the only true power source that can make an eternal difference in your life: Jesus Christ!

GO:

1. What are the areas in your life that war within you and leave you feeling powerless?

2. In what areas are you disciplined off the field of competition?

3. What patterns or habits do you need Christ's help to change?

4. What will you do today to rely on Him and set that change in motion?

WORKOUT:

Job 12:13
Isaiah 40:29–31
Romans 7

R U "FAT"?

"All Scripture is inspired by God and is profitable for teaching, for rebuking, for correcting, for training in righteousness, so that the man of God may be complete, equipped for every good work" (2 Timothy 3:16–17 HCSB).

SET:

I was approached the other day and asked if I was fat. Well, as a former athlete and coach who has put on a few pounds since his glory days, I was taken aback. "I may be fat, but you're ugly," I kidded him. He laughed and responded, "Not that kind of fat!" I was interested to see how he was going to get out of this one.

He went on to tell me that the "fat" he had been talking about stood for Faithful, Available, and Teachable. He told me that we need FAT people involved in sports. What a great thought! We most certainly do need FAT people in every area of life. Athletes need to be FAT. Coaches need to be FAT. Pastors need to be FAT. And the list goes on and on. So I ask: Are you FAT?

Are you faithful to your team? Your family? Your Lord? Are you available to help, serve, or even listen? Are you teachable in your sport? At your school? In your walk with Christ? Are you FAT? As for me, well, I looked in the mirror today, and while I am working on being less fat in stature, but I hope to always be FAT in Christ. My advice: Supersize it! Go large! Make it a Biggie size! Just be FAT for Christ! He needs you to be faithful, available, and teachable for His purposes and His glory.

GO:

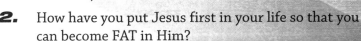

1. Where do you struggle with being faithful, available, and teachable?

2. How have you put Jesus first in your life so that you can become FAT in Him?

3. Where can you be FAT in Christ this week?

WORKOUT:

Psalm 119:30
Proverbs 14:6
Ephesians 3:20

Under the Influence

"Be alert, stand firm in the faith, be brave and strong!"
(1 Corinthians 16:13 HCSB).

SET:

Recently the FCA ministry planned several local events at schools, and I wanted to use the theme "Under the Influence." But shortly after talking to several huddle coaches, I realized that phrase means many different things in our society today. The other coaches lovingly encouraged me to change the theme, and I did.

It can be discouraging to think that the word influence has taken such a negative definition. Today, we are all under the influence of something. Maybe for you it is music or perhaps movies or the internet. As an athlete, maybe it's taking sports-enhancing drugs to make you bigger or better—or it could be following the crowd to parties with alcohol, sex, and drugs. Maybe it is gossip, slander, or just your "stinkin' thinkin'." Whatever the topic, you are under the influence of something today.

Let me suggest some positive influences you can find in today's world:

1. FCA and its ministry—fellowship with other believers and athletes.
2. Daily Christian music. CDs, radio, and even the internet now provide great access to positive Christian music. Check out www.klove com.
3. Your Bible or Christian books and other material.

They can help your faith come alive again.

4. A Christian coach, friend, or pastor who can help to hold you accountable and encourage you daily.
5. A church family to call your own, and growth in truth and knowledge through the fellowship of the church.

My desire—and better yet, God's desire—for you is that you would be under the influence of Jesus Christ. When He is your influence, your attitude will be bright, your outlook better, and your future clearer.

Choose today to be under the influence of Him. But be on your guard; Satan is waiting to trip you up when you least expect it.

Stand up, stand firm, and stand strong...because He is willing and able to give you the strength to use your influence to build His kingdom.

Be encouraged. The influence you are looking for is only a prayer away.

GO:

1. What are you "under the influence" of today?

2. What changes can you make in your life to be under the influence of Christ?

3. Who can you turn to for positive Christian influence?

WORKOUT:

1 Corinthians 16:13
Proverbs 14:6
Ephesians 3:20

T.E.A.M.

Together Everyone Achieves More.

The best football teams I played on in high school, college, and the NFL had one thing in common: These great teams played as a unified, selfless, integrated team. Every player was valuable to the success of the team. The teams understood that together everyone achieves more.

During the 1995-1996 NFL season, I was one of four team captains for the Indianapolis Colts. No one expected much out of us as a team...except the guys in the locker room. As the season progressed, the players began to see that it didn't matter who got their name in the paper or who was interviewed on ESPN's *Sports Center* after a victory. This sacrificial commitment to the "together everyone achieves more" philosophy paid off when the defending Super Bowl Champion San Francisco 49ers came to town. Their roster was crammed with future NFL Hall of Fame players like Jerry Rice and Steve Young. The so-called experts said they would kill us.

T.E.A.M.
BY DERWIN GRAY

For sixty minutes we battled like gladiators.

For sixty minutes we emptied ourselves, believing that together everyone achieves more.

After the sixty minutes expired, we found ourselves victorious at 18–17. And yours truly intercepted Hall of Fame quarterback Steve Young to set a crucial field goal. I was able to make that big momentum-shifting play because my ten teammates on defense were executing their jobs.

Together everyone achieves more.

What I remember most about that game is how every player sensed that what they did mattered...even if they did not play a lot in the game. They knew that throughout the week in practice—as they demonstrated the 49ers offensive, defensive, and special-team plays on scout team—they were actually preparing the men who were going to play a significant portion of the game. We knew that together everyone would achieve more.

That season, a bunch of underestimated men believed that if we played as a unified, selfless, integrated team, we could have a special season. And we did. In the last seconds of the 1995–1996 AFC Championship game, our dream came to an agonizing end. The Pittsburgh Steelers were the better team. But God taught me a lesson of greater value than winning the Super Bowl. He taught me that when people place their individual goals aside and sacrifice for others, together everyone achieves more.

As a disciple of Jesus and as a young pastor, I take this same lesson and apply it to the kingdom of God. When God's people, the church, live as a unified, selfless, integrated team, together everyone achieves more.

Created for Ministry

According to 1 Peter 4:10–11, God has gifted you to serve your local church and community. The living God gives you gifts and even supplies the power to use those gifts to serve others. Why? So God can be made famous through our lives. When you do not use your Spirit-enabled gifts to bless others, it dishonors God and cripples the local church and the community you live in. It also gives you a lack of purpose. America is the land of entertainment, yet many of us are bored with life. Could it be because we are not using our ministry gifts?

You have been born in this time and in your sphere of influence to change the world through the gifts you have been given. You have been gifted for the good of the church and for the sake of the world (1 Corinthians 12:7). If you do not know what your gifts are, ask a mature Christ-follower to help you discover them. The way I discovered my ministry gifts was by volunteering at church. As you serve, your gifts will emerge.

You are a major player on God's team (1 Corinthians 12:14–31). Get in game and make some big plays!

Together everyone achieves more.

T.E.A.M.
BY DERWIN GRAY

Former NFL player Derwin L. Gray (also known as "The Evangelism Linebacker") is the pastor of preaching and spiritual formation of "theGathering," a multi-ethnic, intergenerational equipping church in Charlotte, North Carolina. He also serves as the president of One Heart at a Time Ministries (www.oneheartatatime.org). Derwin's first book, *Hero: Unleashing God's Power in a Man's Heart*, will be releasing in September 2009 from Summerside Press. Derwin lives in North Carolina with his wife, Vicki, and their two children, Presley and Jeremiah.

Identity Crisis

"I am at rest in God alone; my salvation comes from Him" (Psalm 62:1 HCSB).

Athletes are trained to be a certain way. They are trained to be tough, invincible, and strong. Coaches work hard to create identities for their players—but for many of these athletes, once their playing days are over, they struggle to find who they are. They've only ever seen themselves as athletes.

The opening line of the Fellowship of Christian Athletes Competitor's Creed makes a bold statement: "I am a Christian first and last." The identity is stated clearly. I do not read where it says "I am an athlete first and last." No, it says *Christian*—a Christ-follower. Our identity should be found in Christ, not in our sport.

This is easier said than done, and I know from experience. When I finished coaching, I had a rough time at first. I got depressed and angry and was downright rotten to be around, but my self-pity party was interrupted one day when Christ told me I was in the wrong. When I was in His Word, He showed me over and over that sports were what I *did*, not who I *was*. Now my identity is found in Christ. He is who I am. He is who I live for. Not my sports, not my family, not my job, but for Him and Him alone. So when my job, sport, or any other part of my life goes south, I can still rejoice in the One who created me.

If you are struggling from day to day with your identity,

26

look up and smile. The One who created you will be faithful until He calls you home to be with Him. Remember, what you do does not make you who you are!

GO:

1. When have you had an identity crisis? Are you in one now?

2. How does what you do interfere with who God has called you to be in Him?

3. What do you need to change in order to start rooting your identity in Christ?

WORKOUT:

Psalm 61:1–8
Psalm 119:17–20
Colossians 3:2

Black Eyes for Jesus

" 'For God so loved the world that he gave his one and only Son, so that whoever believes in him shall not perish but have eternal life' " (John 3:16 NIV).

John 3:16 is probably the most recognized verse in the entire Bible. Back in 70s and 80s this verse was seen at large sporting events all over the United States. However, recently it has found a home in a different format. College and professional football players now write sayings, area codes, names, and other things on their eye black before games. And throughout the season and bowl games, several college football players made it very clear where they stood spiritually, as well. Tim Tebow, on the biggest stage of college football, donned "JOHN" on one side and "3:16" on the other for a national and worldwide audience to see.

Other athletes in their games wore verses like Philippians 3:14 and Galatians 2:20, but if there was one verse you wished everyone could see and understand, John 3:16 might be that verse. A verse of hope, a verse of promise, a verse of dedication, and a verse of destination, these twenty-seven words are etched into the spiritual DNA of all who believe. But what about those who do not believe yet? It is simply one of the greatest nuggets of truth they will ever find.

During the last National Championship game, viewers

tuned in to see a historical football game between two teams that had never faced each other before—or to see two great quarterbacks do battle—but every time the camera was close to Tim Tebow's helmet, you could not help but read his eyes...his black eyes. As great of a champion as Tebow was that night, the greatest message he showed the world was written on his face. I am so thankful that these young men find new and unique ways of sharing their faith to those they influence. My prayer is that this will continue to grow and we will see more and more "black-eyed" athletes for Jesus!

GO:

1. How do you feel about athletes putting verses on their eye black or shoes during competition?

2. If you could display a verse during a game, what verse would you choose and why?

3. Is there a way you can share your faith that people will notice as you compete or work for Him today?

WORKOUT:

Philippians 3:14
Philippians 4:13
Galatians 2:20
Psalm 91

Game Day

"Jesus said to him, 'Away from me, Satan! For it is written:
"Worship the Lord your God, and serve him only" ' "
(Matthew 4:10 NIV).

SET:

Take a deep breath.... Can you smell it? The air puts a special
swagger in your step.... Today is not any other day—it's game
day! Thoughts and feelings rush through our minds as we wait
for game time to arrive. I can still feel, hear, and see the home
crowd at our basketball season opener as if it was just yesterday.
The band songs, the smell of popcorn in the air, the sounds of
people awaiting what the team would give the crowd...

Every player and coach works for one thing: game day. Game
day is about mental and physical preparation for the battle
ahead. Game day is here now. Let the game begin! Our Lord and
Savior is no stranger to competition. I believe He was extremely
competitive. Actually, He was the all-time, undefeated champion
of love! He competed everyday against His archrival, the prince
of darkness, the scum of the earth, the demon of the depths:
Satan himself. Satan tempted, attacked, and hounded Jesus,
hoping He would break. But He never did.

Satan did not give up. He just moved on to other
prey. Easy targets, weak souls, those who were
ready to give up on the Lord for a piece of
the second-best. Yes, people just like you
and me! You see, teammates, every
day is game day if you follow Jesus
Christ! You have to be ready to
battle the enemy every day

30

just like Christ did. Satan knew He was no match for Jesus—but he knows he can get to us, and he knows where we are weak. When Satan tempted Jesus before He  started his public ministry, Jesus put up with Satan until He had had enough and told him to get out of town. He basically said, "Be gone, Satan, because I am going to serve My God and only My God, period. You got it this time?" Satan got the message quite well, but he is still out there, daily trying to defeat us.

Now, we know the game plan, because we have the playbook of God's Word. We're easily defeated because we take our eyes off our goals and off our Coach and keep them on ourselves. When this happens, we are no match for the evil one. In sports, we prepare to near perfection as game day draws near. Why can't we do that for every day that we face the dark side? Why go to battle with a butter knife when you can have the sword of the Spirit on your side? Let's treat every day as game day for Christ. Just as He battled and won over sin and death, He desires for us to do the same with His help! Game day is here; game day is now! The battle is upon you. Are you ready to fight?

GO:

1. How do you athletically prepare for game day?

2. Do you see every day as a spiritual game day? How can you begin to think this way?

3. What can you do to be prepared every day to battle Satan and his team?

WORKOUT:

Matthew 24:42–51
Romans 13:8–14

Who, Me?

READY:

"Above all else, you must live in a way that brings honor to the good news about Christ. Then, whether I visit you or not, I will hear that all of you think alike. I will know that you are working together and that you are struggling side by side to get others to believe the good news" (Philippians 1:27 CEV).

SET:

Every team needs leaders on and off the field who set the example at practice, in the classroom, and with their friends. Leaders show the way to work in all areas of their lives. Many players do not want that responsibility, but as teammates, all athletes can be leaders. Athletes are under the microscope. People are watching. Peers are watching. Fellow athletes are watching. I encourage athletes when I share with them about being a leader, and I usually get the same response—"Who, me?" They feel that nobody is watching them or cares what they do on or off the field. I beg to differ.

Paul knew this quite well. He understood that as believers in Christ we are called to lead. He challenges us in Philippians to live in such a way that brings honor to Christ daily. And not just to live it, but to show it to others for them to follow, as well. Many believers feel that they are not spiritual leaders, but that's what we are all called to be in Christ. No, you might not be called to lead a church or go to a foreign mission field, but we all have a mission field surrounding us to daily demonstrate Christlike leadership to our sphere of influence.

So the next time you say "Who, me?" to leadership as an athlete or believer, remember that others are watching closely. Don't ruin your opportunity to show leadership by living a life not pleasing to God. The best way to blow your witness is to talk one way and act another. This affects every part of your life as an athlete and a follower of Christ. Worse yet, do not be the person no one wants to follow because of double-standard living. Who, me? Yes, *you*! People want to follow someone who will take them higher than they have ever been before. Be a leader, live the life of truth, and let your actions be ones that people will want to follow!

GO:

1. What leadership qualities do you see in yourself? In what areas are you already leading?

2. What are some ways you have led a double life as an athlete? As a believer?

3. How can you start to lead effectively for Christ today?

WORKOUT:

Exodus 3:11–13
1 Thessalonians 4:1
Proverbs 20:22–24

Lost

" 'What man among you, who has 100 sheep and loses one of them, does not leave the 99 in the open field and go after the lost one until he finds it?' " (Luke 15:4 HCSB).

SET:

Can you guess what 98 percent of all athletes on team rosters have in common? What does the remaining 2 percent have that the others do not? Is it playing ability? Payroll size? Nope. It is simply a matter of location and destination.

In Luke 15, Christ tells three stories of lost items. One, a sheep; another, a coin; and the remaining, a son. All were lost, but none of them realized their situation. The sheep did not realize it was lost until the shepherd found it. The coin was content with where it was until the lady who had lost it found it. Finally, the son knew he was gone, but he did not realize he was lost until he returned home to his father.

So just what is it that separates these team rosters across the country? Only 2 percent of these athletes claim to be "Christian athletes." The rest—the other 98 percent—don't realize they are lost. They may be at the top of their game, drive the nicest cars, or make the most money, but a life without Jesus Christ is a life that is lost. No amount of success can earn eternity. Only by returning to the Good Shepherd or coming back home to the heavenly Father will one realize that they are truly found in Him, Jesus Christ. If you are one of the 2 percent of athletes who know the Light, shine on those who are lost and in the dark. Do not allow them to be lost forever. You have the map, you have the game plan, and you possess the directions to the Savior. Share the information with those in need. They may be lost for now, but don't let them be lost forever.

GO:

1. Who first told you about Christ? When did you start following Him?

2. Do you know someone who is lost? How can you recognize when someone is looking for the way?

3. How can you show the lost the way to Christ today?

WORKOUT:

Luke 15
John 14:6
Jeremiah 29:11–14

What Stinks?

"Whatever is true, whatever is noble, whatever is right, whatever is pure, whatever is lovely, whatever is admirable—if anything is excellent or praiseworthy—think about such things" (Philippians 4:8 NIV).

SET:

I had a point guard who struggled early on with her play and her self-confidence. After beating herself up after a practice, I stood by her and said, "What stinks?" She replied, "My game." I disagreed and said it was her attitude about her game. I told her to stop her "stinkin' thinkin'."

Too many times we tend to think the worst about ourselves or our situations. We tend to find our value in who we are as athletes, not who we are with Christ. When this happens, as it did with this player, our stinkin' thinkin' takes over and our God-pleasing thoughts take a backseat.

Paul reminds us in Philippians that we need to think about things that are noble, right, pure, lovely, admirable, and praiseworthy! Our lives are meant to be pleasing to God. We honor God when we think good things—not bad things. Too much of life is caught up in the negative. Let's focus on the positive for God's glory.

Later in the year, my team was down at the half and playing terribly. After a less-than-positive halftime talk, my team slowly walked out of the locker room and back to the court to warm up. The last player to pass me was this young point guard.

She said to me, "Coach, stop your stinkin' thinkin', 'cause we ain't losing this game!" You know what? She was right. We won! It's good to practice what we preach, but I will save that for another devotional. Let's quit our stinkin' thinkin' and start our positive thinking for kingdom-living!

GO:

1. How often does your attitude carry a less-than-desirable smell?

2. Have you focused much on Philippians 4:8 before?

3. How can you stop your stinkin' thinkin' and start kingdom-living today?

WORKOUT:

Proverbs 15:26
Mark 7:20–22
Psalm 139:16–18

True Worship

"Shout it aloud, do not hold back. Raise your voice like a trumpet. Declare to my people their rebellion and to the house of Jacob their sins. For day after day they seek me out; they seem eager to know my ways, as if they were a nation that does what is right and has not forsaken the commands of its God. They ask me for just decisions and seem eager for God to come near them. 'Why have we fasted,' they say, 'and you have not seen it? Why have we humbled ourselves, and you have not noticed?' " (Isaiah 58:1–3 NIV).

SET:

I know a team that loves to talk the talk but doesn't know how to walk the walk. They look the part, but many of them do not work for the true good of the team. Many are in it just for the status and the look, thinking that they have already arrived. On game day, they are dressed to the hilt. They say the right things and look the part, but when the ball is in play, you find out what they are truly made of and how much they have really prepared themselves for the competition.

Isaiah knew a group of people just like that. They thought they had it going on—putting on their spiritual airs in public. But in private, their lives were totally different. Sure, they fasted and went through the spiritual motions, but that didn't get them very far. Isaiah warned them that going through the motions wouldn't cut it! Living the Christian life is more than punching the time clock at church, FCA, or weekly Bible studies. It is a 24/7 commitment to living,

38

learning, and loving God and knowing Him more. We are fooling and cheating ourselves by doing anything less than that. Is it easy? Absolutely not. It requires 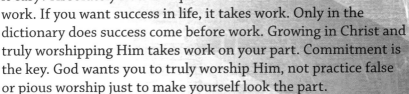 work. If you want success in life, it takes work. Only in the dictionary does success come before work. Growing in Christ and truly worshipping Him takes work on your part. Commitment is the key. God wants you to truly worship Him, not practice false or pious worship just to make yourself look the part.

The team I mentioned earlier has great potential. There are great leaders within, but they need to find out what it means to work together in order to reach the highest goal in their sport. Will they be able to show that they have done what it takes as individuals and the whole, or will they show that they don't know how to walk the walk? Will their lack of work come out in their performances on the field? I am looking forward to finding out. Time will tell. More importantly, as followers of Christ, are we just talking the talk and putting on our spiritual clothes for Sunday? Make a decision today to evaluate your spiritual walk and then walk it! No one wants to follow an idle talker!

GO:

1. How would you describe your work, play, and worship?

2. Are you a talker or a walker?

3. How can you improve your walk with Christ today?

WORKOUT:

John 4:23–24
1 Corinthians 15:58
Hebrews 12:28–29

While in college at Northwestern University, I began to realize that sadness, anxiety, and deep hurt characterized my life. When I was alone, quiet, on my dorm room bed, I would be filled with thoughts of self-hatred, disgust, and shame. My mind would race over every friend and acquaintance, evaluating what they thought of me and how I could favorably manipulate that opinion in the coming day's events. Restlessness overcame my attempts to sleep. Solitude was completely unbearable; I constantly strived to be surrounded by people. My heart was so completely calloused and selfish that even in the tragic death of a college football teammate, I could barely get beyond my own hurt and desired others to pity me, as well. I was passionless in my pursuits and compassionless in all my relationships. I claimed to be a Christian while subtly yet wickedly persecuting the "for real" Christians in my social circle. I despised and maligned most people while desperately desiring their approval at the same time. I felt like a complete mess—an irreparable, sullied, stinking mess.

That is the starting point of my journey into Christianity and Jesus. I'd certainly been to church before. It's rare to find an

PLAYING CHRISTIAN
BY JASON WRIGHT

African American with a praying mother and grandmother who hasn't. Unfortunately, anything that did tug on my heart in our sporadic church stints did not last. Because I had no identity in Jesus, I went through junior high and high school medicated by the latest athletic accomplishment, social honor, counseling session, or good grade through thoughts of depression and suicide. However, once I was in college, the mercy of God no longer allowed my false solutions to sufficiently numb me to my purposeless reality. Finding a purpose for my life was what initially led me to look afresh at my faith. God had sovereignly surrounded me with a number of Christians by my junior year of college. They had passion and drive; a cause to live and to die for. I slowly bought into the hype and found my niche. I decided I would pour all my energy into living a good life, memorizing the Bible, and standing for morality (at least in word if not in deed). Best of all, "real" Christians were very accepting, complimentary, and pleasant. A lot of them were nerdy and socially awkward, making me a very desirable, "cool" addition to the community.

As I progressively steeped myself into Christian circles, a funny thing happened. God began to respond to my vain, religious exercise of praying. Prayers I offered up out of ritual, with a one-hundredth of a mustard seed's hope that it was heard, began to be answered. God began to bless my college football career beyond what I had ever imagined. Academic success and accolades made a roaring comeback in my life. My social status took an exponential leap forward after pledging my fraternity. I was really amazed that God had actually heard my prayers and answered by making my life happy again. The problem (as you can probably tell) was that I had prayed back my false validations and effectively halted my journey into faith.

I was now left in a strange and precarious position. I was shocked that God was far more real than I'd ever thought, but I also felt as though I no longer needed His Christianity to give me comfort. My aching hunger for purpose and significance had been satiated by the resurgence of worldly triumph. Not wanting to risk my newfound success by going into outright rebellion against God, I continued to play the Christian card, saying enough "God stuff" to fool most people and (from what I thought) please God. I led some football team chapel services, prayed every once in a while, and went to a local church when I wasn't too hungover or ashamed of what I'd done the previous night. Heading into my senior year of college, I was reluctantly pulled into a planning meeting for a new group called the Fellowship of Christian Athletes (FCA). I quickly became the point man for this team and began to use all my organization-building expertise to recruit and build it up. Then God threw me a curveball.

As FCA rapidly grew and I oversaw its structural development, something remarkable caught my attention. I began to notice a number of people attending FCA who related to Jesus in a very personal way. They talked about Him as though he were a real person. It was both odd and exciting for me to think of Jesus as more than an abstract concept that justified the way Christians lived in and interpreted the world. As I hung out with that different breed of Christian, I was drawn more and more to the person of Jesus. I began to actually feel convicted

PLAYING CHRISTIAN
BY JASON WRIGHT

about my sin, as if my disobedience did something to God's emotions. I began to have supernatural experiences at the new church I was going to that were deeply personal and could not be ignored. I cannot recall a specific moment of salvation, but in this season of my life (spring through 2003), my journey into Christianity turned into my journey with Jesus.

Fast forward to where I am now: Sporadically ashamed and disgusted; occasionally hating myself; intermittently obsessed with others' opinions; anxious at times; depressed periodically; a sullied, stinking mess. Sounds like paragraph one, doesn't it? However, this time there is so much hope that goes along with this mess of a life. There is so much healing woven into every life experience—the good and the bad. I know Jesus now and am falling deeply in love with Him. And maybe more importantly, I am beginning to feel His love for me. I am starting to hear His loving reply to the deep longings of my heart for real, pure, true love. I am so His now. None of my "growing pains" issues can separate me from Him. I love Him, even in my weakness and immaturity, and He loves me back. In all of my messes, He loves me back.

Jason Wright was an All-American running back from Northwestern University. He won the first Bobby Bowden FCA Player of the Year while at Northwestern. He has been in the NFL for six years (with Atlanta, Cleveland, and Arizona). Jason has been the spiritual leader on the teams he has played for.

Where Is Your Heart?

"For where your treasure is, there your heart will be also"
(Matthew 6:21 HCSB).

SET:

It was Christmas 1973; everything was good with the world.
Northern Indiana snow, family and friends, time to open
presents... I had only one wish that year: to get a basketball. And
I couldn't have been happier when my wish came true with a
brand-new Wilson. It quickly became my treasure. I would play
nonstop—inside, outside, hot, or cold. It was just me and my
ball. I honestly had no desire to do much of anything else other
than to shoot and play imaginary games in which I won any and
every championship. My heart was hooked on hoops.

In Matthew 6, Jesus teaches us to not store up treasures on
this earth where thieves can steal and rust can decay; rather, we
should store up treasures in heaven and long for the day when
we enter His presence. Today, our treasures vary from person to
person. For some, it is home, family, or friends; for others it is
a car or other material possessions. Still others treasure things
like physical appearance. One only needs to look
at his or her calendar or checkbook to see their
treasures. Our treasures get our time,
money, and hearts.

Even though my basketball
wore out, my love for the game
never did. As I graduated from
college and began coaching,

basketball was still my treasure. I was a Christian, but my top priority was basketball. It took the birth and death of my third child for me to understand that I was storing up treasure in the wrong things and places. My son, through his life, taught me that eternity is where my heart should be.

I would love to say that I have it all figured out regarding where my heart should be, but I sometimes get off track. My time, my money, my thoughts, and my heart are not always Christ-centered. But my prayer is that we all would ponder the paths of our feet and number of our days, keeping the first things first: our faith in Christ and the perspective of Him as Lord and Savior.

I still love basketball, but I do my best to make sure it is a distant second to my pursuit of Christ. Today, take some time to evaluate your treasures. Ask yourself, "Where is my heart?"

GO:

1. What is the top priority in your life?

2. Make a list of the things you put in front of your relationship with Christ. Pray about each one and ask God to give you guidance regarding how to change your heart.

3. How can you make Jesus Christ and God's Word your treasure today?

WORKOUT:

2 Chronicles 16:9
Psalm 90:12
Proverbs 4:26

Honor Him

"Therefore, fear the LORD and worship Him in sincerity and truth. Get rid of the gods your ancestors worshiped beyond the Euphrates River and in Egypt, and worship the LORD" (Joshua 24:14 HCSB).

SET:

The sports world loves to pay tribute to great athletes and coaches. Halls of Fame, retired jerseys and retired numbers, street names and building names—all to honor famous sports heroes. But what are they really honoring? Some were great men and women off the field, but for the most part those things honor great achievements in athletics. In my book there's nothing wrong with that, until we look at whether we truly honor Christ in our sporting endeavors.

As athletes, how do we honor the Lord? Do we honor Him with our words? With our daily practice ethics? With our personal integrity? Honoring Christ is just as much an on-field endeavor as an off-field one. Are you an athlete or a Christian? Which one are you truly trying to be? Believe it or not, you *can* be both at the same time.

Joshua understood this quite well. He was a fierce leader and competitor, but he told people where he truly stood. Joshua knew that his life was supposed to honor the Lord and that he should serve Him with everything he had. He knew he needed to be both a leader and a Christian at the same time in order to give his life meaning and purpose.

Where does that leave you? Do you battle to combine your faith and your sport? If so, why? Christ doesn't want you to leave your sport, but He does want you to compete fiercely for Him and for His honor and glory. So I ask you this: Are you trying to honor Christ or yourself in your sport? If we honor Christ as we play, we will act differently, talk differently, and live differently, but that doesn't mean we have to play with less intensity.

Today, be like Joshua! Honor Christ and serve Him with all you are. Play for Him! Honor Him with all that you have! You can do it!

GO:

1. How do you honor Christ in your sport?

2. Do you honor Christ off the field?

3. How can you bring more glory and honor to Christ today?

WORKOUT:

Psalm 86:12
Mark 12:30
1 Peter 2:11–12

The Right Path

"So follow the way of good people, and keep to the paths of the righteous" (Proverbs 2:20 HCSB).

SET:

It was the biggest race of the season. All the runners were ready to go. The rugged course was full of hills and rough terrain, but it was *the* race of the year. Every runner was excited to get started. With a single shot, the runners raced toward the opening in the woods. Early in the race, seven runners broke from the pack and came to a fork in the path. The lead runner made the choice, and each runner followed in stride.

In sports today, there are leaders and followers. Some leaders set a great example, but others struggle to make the right decisions, thus leading others astray. They may be leaders, but they are leading their teammates down the wrong paths. Many young athletes are very impressionable. They are looking for leadership above them and will follow those leaders on and off the floor. It takes an athlete who is strong in mind, body, and spirit to discern the right path to follow. Most can easily be led the wrong way. We need to apply today's verse and follow those who stay on the right path both on and off the field of competition.

As the seven runners blazed down the path, they realized that they were running the wrong way. This mistake caused all seven to finish at the back of the pack, thus losing the big race.

Today, ask yourself whom you are following. What path are

they taking you down? Is yours the straight and narrow path of the righteous or the wide road to destruction? If you are on the wrong path, turn around! Head back in the other direction. It is *never* too late to turn around and go the right way! Once you are on the right path, continue to follow it until you reach your goal...your heavenly goal.

GO:

1. Is someone leading you astray? How?
2. Are you leading others down the wrong path?
3. What path are you currently on, and where will it eventually lead?
4. Today, how can you start and stay on the right path of life?

WORKOUT:

Proverbs 2
Matthew 5:16
Matthew 7:13–14

The Voice of Truth

"Teach me Your way, LORD, and I will live by Your truth"
(Psalm 86:11 HCSB).

I love sports movies, and my all-time favorite is "Hoosiers." That might have something to do with my being a former Indiana high school basketball player, and the movie was filmed in the 80s when I was in college. One scene from the movie stood out to me. During one game, Hickory (the high school) was in need of a sub, and the coach didn't have anyone to put in the game except Ollie, the manager. So Coach put him in late, and Ollie got fouled and had to go to the line for two free throws. The crowd was yelling, the opposing team was taunting, and Ollie's knees were shaking as he stepped to the line.

Throughout the Bible's history, men and women heard voices of opposition but chose to listen to the Voice of Truth. Let's look at several examples. What if Moses had listened to Pharaoh or all the grumblings of the Israelites as they traveled? What if Joshua had listened to those who said they only needed to go around Jericho six times? What if David had listened to everyone who said he was too little, too young, and too weak to defeat Goliath? And what if Esther had not been brave enough to go to the king, her husband, and beg on behalf of her people? The outcome of each would have been different. These people, however, and many more throughout history, listened to the Voice of Truth—the voice of God pouring truth into their lives. This

Voice of Truth is still alive and well today.

Back to our story... Ollie stepped up to the line. In the middle of the cries of opposition, he nailed the first free throw. The other team called a time-out to "ice" him. But during the time-out, the coach said that "*after* Ollie hits the free throw," they would run a certain defense. The coach was a confident voice of truth at that moment in Ollie's life. Ollie stepped up and nailed the next free throw, and Hickory won the game to advance.

The popular singing group Casting Crowns sings of this Voice of Truth in a song by that title. One phrase in the song says it all: "Out of all the voices calling out to me, I will choose to listen and believe the Voice of Truth." We all have voices of opposition in our lives. Satan wants to see us fail, and he won't stop trying. He'll use many different strategies to keep us from growing in our faith. However, there is one voice that rings louder and truer than any voice I know: God's voice, found especially in His Word and in prayer.

GO:

1. Which voice do you hear in your life today? Are you listening to the right voice?

2. What does the Voice of Truth sound like to you? What do the voices of opposition sound like?

3. How much time do you spend in the Word or in prayer to be able to hear the Voice of Truth?

WORKOUT:

Psalm 29:3–4
Psalm 66:18–20

God's Playbook

"Direct my footsteps according to your word; let no sin rule over me" (Psalm 119:133 NIV).

SET:

Most sports have a playbook or set of rules to follow in their program—something that tells how things will be done on and off the field for success in the system. I recently heard one coach refer to his playbook as his "bible." Obviously, he highly values the book.

As we read through Psalm 119, we find many verses that reference God's Word. Although David appears to be one if not *the* main contributor of the book of Psalms, it is actually a compilation of writings from several authors—yet even among this varied authorship, we find it repeated many times that God's Word guided the writer. They understood that God's Word was the only playbook they could follow that could give true, absolute direction for life.

When I coached basketball, my playbook was very important to me. However, it did not take precedence over the real Playbook of my life. Only God's Word can give ultimate direction. My basketball playbook could say which play to run in what situation, but only during the games. God's Word gives us direction every day, for every situation, in everything that comes our way.

GO:

1. Where do you go for direction?

2. Does God's Word guide your steps, or are you marching to a different beat?

3. How can you start to make the Bible your ultimate road map today?

WORKOUT:

Psalm 119:11, 73, 105

The Hot List

"Six things the LORD hates; in fact, seven are detestable to Him: arrogant eyes, a lying tongue, hands that shed innocent blood, a heart that plots wicked schemes, feet eager to run to evil, a lying witness who gives false testimony, and one who stirs up trouble among brothers" (Proverbs 6:16–19 HCSB).

SET:

There are some things that just set off a coach. Together those things make up what I call my "Hot List"—things that made me mad fast!

1. A lazy player.
2. Someone who is constantly late.
3. Those who would rather complain than try harder.
4. Those who blame everyone else and never take responsibility for their own actions.

Players like that really pushed me to the limit as a coach. Was there redeeming value in them? Absolutely. But rarely did they see it in themselves.

Many coaches have a "Hot List," and theirs may include more things than what I listed. But did you know that the Lord has a list as well? It includes arrogance, deceit, evil thoughts and actions, grumbling, and more. And what's more, the Lord says He won't put up with it. Sure, He is patient, kind, and loving, but He is also fair, just, and a God of discipline. The

more you know and love God, the
more you will want to stay away
from His "Hot List" sins.

There are many things that
are out of a player's control both on
and off the court, but there are also many things they *can*
control. As a player, learn what sets your coach off and then strive
to work in a way that will give God the glory and honor above
all else. If you do this in all things, you will surely stay out of the
doghouse, and those "Hot List" items will rarely, if ever, enter
your mind. My greatest advice to you today? Keep Jesus first, and
everything will find its proper place!

GO:

1. How and when have you pushed your coach to the edge
with your attitudes and actions?

2. Which of the seven things that the Lord hates have you
engaged in?

3. How can you start keeping Jesus first in everything?

WORKOUT:

Proverbs 6
Matthew 6:33
Mark 12:30

Never Forget

"So his fame spread even to distant places, for he was marvelously helped until he became strong. But when he became strong, he grew arrogant and it led to his own destruction. He acted unfaithfully against the LORD his God by going into the LORD's sanctuary to burn incense on the incense altar" (2 Chronicles 26:15—16 HCSB).

SET:

We know them well. Athletes who, at first, worked hard and gave the credit to God for their success. But then as success came, more and more, they gave God the glory less and less. We see it happen all the time—the once-humble athlete asking for more of the world and less of God. Pride takes over!

King Uzziah was one of these men. Under the spiritual influence of Zechariah, Uzziah sought the Lord and was blessed in his pursuit of Him. This blessing was taken to heart—the wrong heart. Uzziah started to focus more on himself and less on what God had done for him. He quickly became powerful, and he just as quickly forgot what (or who) got him to that point. He even began ignoring his spiritual mentor. Who needed Zechariah? Uzziah was on top of the world! He became so proud and brash that he even entered the temple and tried to do things only the priests were allowed to do. It became all about him.

God has a way of bring people to their knees. Remember, pride always comes before a fall. Uzziah's fall began when his disobedience led to leprosy. This disease led to

56

his spiritual and ultimate defeat. God reminded Uzziah every day through his leprosy, "Never forget, I am still *the* Man!"

Have you forgotten who the Man truly is? Too many of us today say, "You're the man" to each other and puff out our chests. We reek of pride! But lest we forget, we are only human. Only He is *the* Man. Never forget who created you and why He did it: so you would serve Him and live to glorify Him in all you do. Oh yeah, and give credit where credit is due... lest you break out with an unknown rash on your forehead.

GO:

1. What are you prideful about? Has pride taken over your life?

2. How can you remain humble?

3. How can you start to remember what God has done for you today?

WORKOUT:

2 Chronicles 26
Psalm 101:5
Proverbs 8:13; 11:2; 16:5, 18

GET REAL WITH GOD

Rolf Kamper

Even though I was born and raised in the Lutheran Church and had a very strict upbringing, God did not truly become real in my life until one night during my freshman year of college.

Growing up, I attended church services and Sunday school every week and also took part in confirmation classes every Wednesday night. I did not understand then why my parents were so strict and made me do the things they did, but now, as an adult, I realize that I have been very blessed by the strong morals and beliefs they instilled in me.

When I was a kid, my parents placed two things in my hand: a Bible and a basketball. At the time, I only accepted the latter of the two. I rebelled when it came to church; I would often not want to get up on Sunday mornings to go to service or do the weekly homework that was required for confirmation classes. I was educated when it came to God; I knew all the Bible stories and the proper ways a Christian is supposed to act. But I was lacking the most important thing:

KEEPING CHRIST #1
BY DREW NEITZEL

a true relationship with God. Maybe this was by choice, or maybe I just didn't understand how to go about it then. To me, the only thing that was important was playing basketball and trying to make it into the NBA someday. My life was basketball, period.

I thought my life was perfect in those days. My father taught me that the only way to reach my goals was through hard work, so that's what I did. I worked hard in the classroom and even harder on the basketball court. I was obsessed with success, and it was all around me at a young age. I felt like I was in control of everything and could do anything I wanted in life. Life was going great for me. I accepted a scholarship to play basketball at Michigan State University as a sophomore in high school and was having success in every part of my life until the day I first set foot on the campus of Michigan State.

As freshman, we were required to take summer classes before starting our first semester in the fall, so we could get acclimated to the college lifestyle. Life was not so easy anymore, with moving away from home, performing the intense workouts of college, waking up at 6 a.m. to run and lift, going to class all day, practicing at night, doing homework, and then repeating it all over again the next day. I remember even finding it hard to sit down for twenty minutes to eat lunch.

With the increased workload both on and off the court, I began dealing with the pressures that go along with being a high-profile college athlete—as well as the many temptations on a college campus. I struggled a lot with these things during my first year. It was difficult going from high school where I was "the man" to being a college freshman and the low man on the totem pole. I couldn't handle the stresses of everyday life anymore, and I just wanted to give up.

This was when God stepped in and became "real" in my life. I remember the day so clearly. I was lying in my bed late one night, listening to music, and I said to myself, "Something needs to change. I don't know if this is right for me. I don't know if I can handle this every day for the next four years." At that moment I closed my eyes and prayed, "Lord, come into my life today and lift these stresses and burdens off my chest. I need you more than anything, God. Guide me and walk with me on my journey, Lord. I have realized that I cannot do this alone. Help me to put my faith in you, Lord, as I know you have a wonderful plan in store for me."

As I was praying to God that night, I began to cry. It was the strangest thing. As an athlete, I was taught to be tough and not show weakness, but I could not hold back the tears. I was weak—weak when I tried to do things my way—but I then realized I could be strong and nothing could get me down with God on my team. That was the moment in my life when I knew that God was listening to my prayer and that He was going to be there for me through everything.

When I woke up the next morning, I felt like a new

KEEPING CHRIST #1
BY DREW NEITZEL

person. I felt as if I could accomplish anything in life—not by myself as when I was younger, but with God on my side and in control of my life. From that moment forward, my relationship has grown each day with Him. Just like everyone else, I go through ups and downs in my life as well as in my faith and relationship with God. Sometimes, as athletes, when we have a lot of success, we feel we can do it on our own again, and we forget to give God the glory. That is when God pulls us back to Him...when we start to slide off the path He has set for us. I now live each and every day to glorify Him, both on and off the court. Basketball is still very important to my life, as it was when I was growing up, but my relationship with God is number one now.

Drew Neitzel is a former NCAA All-American from the Michigan State Spartans. He was a four-year starter for the basketball team. He is currently playing professional basketball in Germany and consistently shares his faith with his teammates and the people in Germany. His goal is to make to the NBA.

Awesome

"For the LORD Most High is awesome. He is the great King of all the earth" (Psalm 47:2 NLT).

SET:

The word *awesome* is used to describe so much in sports today. "Did you see that awesome catch?" "What about that awesome dunk?" "That home run was awesome!" I looked up this word in the Urban Dictionary. It defines *awesome* as "totally cool." It is what is called a "sticking plaster" word, which is something used by Americans to cover the huge gaps in our vocabulary. It is supposedly one of three words that make up most American sentences. And in sports today, that is definitely the case. Everything great is "awesome."

I'm afraid that we are misusing this word, however. It may be that this special word should really be reserved for God alone. It should be set apart for the One who is like no other and who will never be repeated. Let's take a look in God's Word to see what *awesome* really means. Isaiah 40:12 describes the awesomeness of God with these questions: "Who else has held the oceans in his hand? Who has measured off the heavens with his fingers? Who else knows the weight of the earth or has weighed the mountains and hills on a scale?" (NLT). Also, the first sentence in the Bible speaks of God's awesomeness: "In the beginning God created the heavens and the earth" (NLT). What more do you need?

There are amazing catches, great plays, and fantastic finishes to games, but all of them have been repeated in some way,

62

shape, or form. Only God has been unrepeated. There is no one like our God (see 1 Samuel 2:2). So when you are watching something (sports, movies, TV, whatever), call it what it is, but don't call it *awesome* unless it is about God. Work on reserving that word for the only One worthy of its acclaim. There are some things that should only ever be for Him. The word *awesome* should be on that list. Why? Because He is an awesome God!

GO:

1. How do you tend to use the word *awesome*?

2. How is God awesome in your life?

3. How can you reflect on God's awesome power today and apply it to your daily pursuits?

WORKOUT:

1 Chronicles 17:20
Psalm 99:3
Isaiah 40

The Eyes
of the Lord

READY:

"For the eyes of the LORD run to and fro throughout the whole earth, to give strong support to those whose heart is blameless toward him" (2 Chronicles 16:9 ESV).

SET:

One day the team was practicing, when their coach had to leave for a minute. Once the coach was out of sight, the team started acting up and shooting half-court shots. Suddenly, out of nowhere, they heard a voice say, "I saw that." One player made the comment, "Man, Coach must have eyes everywhere." In sports, the eyes of a coach are always watching even when no one thinks they are looking.

The eyes of the Lord are always watching as well. God's Word is very clear about how God is watching us. Why does He watch over us? He loves us too much not to. But I know that many still struggle with the fact that God is watching. Some see His attentiveness as His not wanting anything good to happen to us. Others look at it as though He is playing good cop/bad cop. Still others feel as if He is always trying to catch them doing something bad. These are wrong impressions of God. The eyes of the Lord watch us because He loves us.

How does it make you feel, knowing that the eyes of the Lord are watching you? As we live for Christ, it should give us confidence that He cares about us.

Throughout God's Word, we read about those who found favor in the eyes of the Lord and others who did evil. When God watches you, what does He see?

Like the coach who always seems to see everything, our God does see everything, and His eyes are looking for those who want to follow Him.

GO:

1. How does it make you feel to know that God is watching over you?

2. God sees the good, the bad, and the ugly in our lives. When do you wish He was not watching?

3. What is the positive side of His seeing us during our sinful behavior?

WORKOUT:

Genesis 6:8
Psalm 34:15
Proverbs 5:21; 15:3
1 Peter 3:12

Slump

"They wander about for food and howl if not satisfied. But I will sing of your strength, in the morning I will sing of your love; for you are my fortress, my refuge in times of trouble" (Psalm 59:15–16 NIV).

SET:

Tiger Woods went a month without winning a tournament. Barry Bonds didn't homer for a week. Jeff Gordon didn't win a race for a month. These are all true career stories of the great athletes named. Sportswriters love reporting stories like these because they get to go for the jugular. They break out the big "S" word—*slump*. Sports fans and writers get used to sports heroes performing day in and day out. When the reality hits that these athletes aren't perfect, people feel as if they have to make an excuse or that something must be terribly wrong with the athlete in question. For the three examples above, I'm not sure that the word "slump" is right, but we all go through tough times in life and in sport.

Webster defines *slump* as a "slide," a "decline," or a "falling off." I can relate to the word *slump*. Recently it appeared that I was in one. I was allowing life to get the best of me. Everything in life was starting to slide...work, home, and church. I didn't want to write or even do much of anything. I was in a spiritual slump, too. Why? I'm not really sure, but I didn't have to hit a three-hundred-yard drive, a game-winning homer, or race five hundred miles at 200 mph to get out of my slump.

I simply turned my head toward heaven and asked for help. I had lost my joy, my happiness, my way home. I had taken my eyes off Him and concentrated on myself—but God reminded me just how good I really had it with Him and in Him. After reading the passage in Psalm 59, He showed me, as He *always* does, that His love is more than enough to sustain me and keep me happy in Him.

Are you in a slump in sport, in life, or in spirit? If so, take courage and take hold of His truth for you today. He is our refuge in times of distress, and we can shout for joy every day because of His unfailing love. Slump? What slump? God is the ultimate slump-breaker. Allow Him to help today. He works if you give Him a chance!

GO:

1. Ever feel like you are in a slump, athletically or spiritually?

2. Are you currently on a spiritual upswing or downslide?

3. How can you start to find joy in Jesus and break out of the funk?

WORKOUT:

Matthew 6:33
Romans 15:13
Hebrews 12:1–3

What Do You Want from Me?

" 'And now, Israel, what does the LORD your God require of you? He requires only that you fear the LORD your God, and live in a way that pleases him, and love him and serve him with all your heart and soul. And you must always obey the LORD's commands and decrees that I am giving you today for your own good' " (Deuteronomy 10:12–13 NLT).

SET:

Luke had the potential to be a good player, but he got so frustrated with his game. He did not understand why his coach always wanted him to change his shot and other parts of his game. He finally had a talk with his coach, and things suddenly became clearer to him. His improvement took off. Coach simply told Luke what he needed to do to get better and how it would help him in years to come.

As Moses was leading the people of Israel through the wilderness, many started to grumble and complain. Though God continued to provide for their needs, they soon forgot His provisions. God gave Moses the guidelines to live by, and Moses constantly shared them with his people. I can picture someone approaching Moses and saying, "What does He [God] want from me?" Moses summarized God's desire with these verses in Deuteronomy, sharing four things: fear Him, live for Him, love Him, and serve Him. Everything we do is encompassed by these things.

Have you ever felt like Luke? I know I have, both athletically and spiritually. When I read these verses again, God opened my heart to understand them in a better way. If you are struggling with what God wants from you, spend some time in these verses, too. See where the Lord needs you to grow and get "One Day Better" in Him. I hope they will bless your heart as much as they recently have mine.

GO:

1. When was a time you struggled with what someone expected or required from you? What was the outcome?

2. How are you doing in the four areas indicated from today's verses?

3. Today, in which of these four areas will you make a greater effort to grow?

WORKOUT:

Mark 12:30–31
1 Thessalonians 4:1–3
Romans 14:12–13

Fear Factor

"Now this is what the LORD says—the One who created you, Jacob, and the One who formed you, Israel—'Do not fear, for I have redeemed you; I have called you by your name; you are Mine'" (Isaiah 43:1 HCSB).

SET:

John stepped up to the plate. The bases were loaded with two outs, and his team was down by one run. You could tell he was nervous. How would John respond? *Strike one!* He watched it go by. *Strike two!* He watched another. *Strike three!* The bat never left John's shoulder. John returned to the dugout and was approached by his coach. "You never even took a swing. Why not?" John replied, "I thought you would be mad if I struck out swinging."

This happens a lot in sports. Fear grips an athlete. Fear of a coach, fear of failure, fear of losing... Whatever the fear may be, fear is a factor in sports today—and in life, as well.

In many Christian homes across the country, fear is being taught. And not the good kind of respectful fear, but the kind that can make a person timid and afraid. Faith can become so legalistic that fear grips the hearts of young and old. Christ did not come to earth to instill fear but to give freedom from it. Pastors may preach fear and parents may instill fear, because, after all, being fearful is not necessarily a bad thing. But Christ does not intend for us to live in fear. He intends for us to live in the freedom that we can find in Him.

70

What fear grips your life? Maybe it is the fear of not being forgiven. Maybe it's the fear that God's grace is not enough for you or the fear that God's love does not include you. *Fear not*, friends. Just as good coaches do not intend to make their players fearful of them, God also does not intend for you to live in fear—but in freedom from sin and death by living for Him. Fear does not need to be a factor in your athletic world or in your life with Christ. Remember, He has called you, and you are His forever.

GO:

1. What do you fear when you compete? In what ways could a coach cause you fear?

2. How do you have freedom from sin in your life?

3. How can you start today to live free from fear as a child of God?

WORKOUT:

Jeremiah 29:11–14
Daniel 10:19
Hebrews 13:6

The Good, the Bad, and the Ugly

"Whatever happens, conduct yourselves in a manner worthy of the gospel of Christ" (Philippians 1:27 NIV).

Does this sound familiar? "The ref made me mad, so I had to say it!" Or maybe this one: "It's not my fault I got a tech; did you see what he did to me?" We've all been there. We've all let our attitudes and anger control our actions and achievements. Then we play the justification game. We've learned that it is never *our* fault but usually a teammate's, an opposing player's, or the coach's. When I coached, I was constantly reminded of how I acted in tough situations during the game with officials. Was I being Christlike in my walk and talk during the game? Many times I failed to reach the mark.

Paul was a great example of how to conduct oneself during tough times. Paul was beaten, thrown into jail, and almost killed on many occasions, but he constantly maintained an attitude of gratitude. He stated in Philippians that we need to conduct ourselves in a way that will honor Christ by what we do and say—no matter what happens.

So when things don't go your way, whether on or off the court, do you let your attitude control your altitude with Christ? Whatever happens, whether the good, bad, or ugly in life, make Jesus Christ proud of your response to the situation.

When your way doesn't work...
look to Yahweh!

GO:

1. When has your attitude affected your altitude with Christ?

2. When has your way gotten in the way of God's way for you?

3. Is your conduct worthy or worthless?

WORKOUT:

1 Thessalonians 4:1
Romans 14:12–13
Romans 6:11–13

Heart of a Competitor

"The godly walk with integrity; blessed are their children who follow them" (Proverbs 20:7 NLT).

Ready...Set...Go—and they were off! Sixty junior-high cross-country runners, heading for the first hill. They ran all over the park—a 1.5-mile course through woods, hills, and around playgrounds. Jay, a seventh-grade boy, was leading the field about halfway through the race. As they turned for the woods, Jay and the runner behind him approached a turn. Jay went on one side of the cone, his competitor the other. The race continued...but Jay turned around.

Integrity is a word that many use today but few truly understand. It is defined as moral character, honesty, and soundness throughout. David, in his psalms, emphasizes integrity and relates it to the heart. Integrity is a heart issue and affects everything we do. Integrity is doing the right thing when no one is looking. That's a big challenge for all of us to follow.

Jay had turned around because he believed he went on the wrong side of the cone. As he backtracked, his competitor distanced himself from Jay and the rest of the runners. Jay knew he needed to do the right thing. He was raised by godly parents who taught that, no matter what the cost, you always do the right thing. Jay used tremendous energy to get back up to second place after many runners passed him during his detour. He battled until the final turn and raced for the finish line. He did not win the race, as he was beaten by a teammate in the last ten yards, but he did finish third. After the race Jay would say, "I wanted to stop and cry because I knew I had made a wrong turn, but I could not give up." Jay's effort may not have won him the race, but his character and integrity showed many people the true heart of a competitor for Christ.

Jay made the right choice at the right time in the right place. Can you say the same? Coach isn't watching, but are you going hard at it?... The office will never miss that extra paper or materials, you think, as you slide them into your backpack.... Mom and Dad aren't home so I can do whatever I want on the computer.... These may all happen daily, but remember that there is always Someone watching and waiting for you to make the right choice at the right time in the right place. Christ's desire is for you to do the right thing. Show the heart of a competitor and do not give into temptation. Live to win. Your integrity is at stake.

GO:

1. When have you had to make a decision like Jay's?

2. How would someone say your integrity measures up?

3. How are you living today for God in what you do, say, and think?

WORKOUT:

Psalm 25:21
Romans 5:4
Deuteronomy 8:2

For Lorenzo Romar, *integrity* is one of the simplest concepts he's ever learned—so simple that it only takes a brief, pondering pause followed by a concisely spoken sentence for him to explain it.

"A person with integrity consistently does the right thing," he states matter-of-factly.

As the men's basketball coach at the University of Washington, Romar has provided a walking, talking example of integrity to the young athletes that don the Huskies uniform year-in and year-out.

Take, for example, the coach's no-swearing policy. During practices and games, players are not allowed to use any form of profanity. If they do, the penalty is a healthy number of laps around the court. Romar says it's not even a spiritual matter, necessarily, but rather an issue of self-control and class.

"What I've found is that guys will not use cuss words around me off the court, either, but I've never told them [not to do] that," Romar says. " 'Off the court,' I've told them, 'that's your life. But on the court, when people are watching how we conduct ourselves, that's disrespectful to some and offends some, so stay away from it.' "

Romar's strong disciplinarian style is in sharp contrast to much of what he experienced growing up in Compton—the famed rough-and-tumble Los Angeles community. All around him were signs of family breakdown, but Romar—who says he wouldn't want to have grown up anywhere else—is thankful for his parents, who raised him in a household built on integrity.

"There was crime and some other things that weren't good, but I did my best to stay away from those things," Romar says. "I couldn't come home if I did something I had no business doing. I also had a desire to be something special in this sport, and I knew that the other peripheral things could get me off track, so there was no interest in them at all."

One of Romar's favorite scriptures is Ephesians 5:1, which admonishes believers to "Be imitators of God" (NIV).

"If I can keep that perspective, I am basically living out a script as if I were an actor," Romar says. "I'm not talking about being phony, [just that] I've taken on a different attitude, a different outlook. I see everything through that outlook as I'm guided by my coach or my producer—[who] is Christ—as opposed to my own views, my fleshly, worldly views."

Romar says that when the temptation to cave in to his own humanity is strong, he immediately reminds himself of the damage such a moral failure would do to his witness and any future opportunities he might have to share the gospel. He also relies heavily on the prompting of the Holy Spirit, which helps to keep him accountable to the Christ-centered life of integrity.

"There have been times when I've made mistakes," Romar admits. "I'm not perfect. But I'm aware of those mistakes, and I'm miserable when I have made mistakes. That's a big, big difference between a man with integrity and a Christian with integrity. I think you can be a man of integrity without being a Christian and not feel guilty when you do it your way. If you've got the Spirit of God living in you, man, you're going to be miserable if you don't do it His way.

"The best way to go through life is to be a man of integrity," Romar concludes. "Living a life of integrity does not mean you're missing out on anything. You're not. You're actually going to discover the fun part of life. Integrity is ultimately being a man of God."

Coach Lorenzo Romar is the head coach of the University of Washington. A former college and NBA player, Romar is known for his toughness and hard work. His faith is evident throughout his coaching, both on and off the floor, as he shares with groups across the country.

INTEGRITY

Damaging Words

"Likewise the tongue is a small part of the body, but it makes great boasts. Consider what a great forest is set on fire by a small spark" (James 3:5 NIV).

SET:

Have you ever turned a television channel to a ball game, watched as the camera zeroed in on the bench during a tough moment, and witnessed a coach or player saying words he shouldn't have said? Foul language is commonplace in athletics today. What makes the use of these words so attractive? Some say it motivates; others say it is necessary to get the point or lesson across. If that is the case, how do teachers and preachers give lessons of life without using these words? If this type of language is used to motivate, then why is over 90 percent of it used in a negative context?

In the New Testament, James shares that the tongue is a very dangerous weapon. Controlling our speech is vitally important in our spiritual journey. Often we are judged not by what we do, but by what comes out of our mouths. I've heard it said, "Swearing is the expression of a weak mind trying to express itself forcibly," and I think that's the best definition of swearing yet. I have not met an athlete or coach who would admit to having a weak mind, but such language might speak for itself. Great coaches now and in the past have had great success without using harsh language. Coach John Wooden is a good example of this. What can we learn from him? I am sure that controlling the tongue meant controlling other areas in their coaching (i.e. anger and attitude), as well.

Many athletes have said that swearing is a difficult habit to break, but guarding your tongue is a discipline that needs to be practiced just like the skills in your sport. Athletes, does swearing make you a better player? Have you considered the damage your words can do to your teammates and others around you? If not, stop right now and consider what would happen if you stopped swearing today and used different words to convey your message. Clean up the talk and see what happens. If you don't use foul language, good for you. Let your teammates know it bothers you, as well. Be the first on your team to take a stand in this important area. I guarantee you will see the difference.

GO:

1. When do you find yourself struggling with foul language?

2. When your language goes south, what goes along for the ride? Your anger, as well?

3. Today, how can you start to tame the tongue and use words that will not offend others?

WORKOUT:

James 3:1–12
Matthew 5:37

Proper Preparation

"After fasting forty days and forty nights, he [Jesus] was hungry" (Matthew 4:2 NIV).

How do you prepare for a game? For a season? For a test? Do you spend time making a game plan that will work, or do you just hope for the best? While watching teams play over the years in many different sports, one begins to wonder. Some teams work their plans to perfection, but you wonder if others just roll out the balls in practice while the coach takes a nap. Now, we know that never happens; preparing for a contest or upcoming season takes much time in being devoted to the necessary details before a team is ready to compete. When the final day comes, before the games begin, will the team be able to put into practice what they worked so hard at perfecting? Physically, they may be ready, but what about mentally, or better yet, spiritually? Spiritually prepared? Yes—God does care how you prepare to compete and perform in action and in attitude.

Jesus Himself had to prepare for battle and competition, even though His foe was no match. Before Jesus began His earthly ministry, He was led into the wilderness by the Holy Spirit to be tempted by Satan. In order to prepare, Jesus ate nothing for forty days and nights. Jesus knew His task. He studied and knew his opponent well. He took away any distractions that could possibly hinder His singular focus for His life. What a game plan! By fasting in preparation for His work on earth, Jesus focused solely on following God's plan for His life. Even though the temptation to follow other plans was given immediately after His time of fasting and preparation, He was steadfast and true, showing not only that He truly was the Son of God, but that true strength and spiritual readiness come only from the Father in heaven!

As you prepare to play, I am certainly not suggesting that you fast for forty days and nights, but I am suggesting that you follow Christ's example by being prepared spiritually for competition so you'll be able to withstand the testing and trials of life and sport. Will you follow the game plan of the team to the end or give in when the first trial or temptation comes along?

GO:

1. What is one weak area of your preparation?

2. Do you consider it important to be spiritually ready to compete?

3. What can you do to better prepare for competing in sport and life?

WORKOUT:

Ephesians 6:10–18
2 Timothy 4:2

Getting Cut: A Good Thing?

READY:

"And we know that in all things God works for the good of those who love him, who have been called according to his purpose" (Romans 8:28 NIV).

SET:

By the third preseason game of an NFL team, many players find out where they stand in trying to make the cut. One such player, Jason, found out some bad news. Before his third game, he was told that he had been cut. Jason drove home, obviously disappointed in not making the team.

At times we don't understand why God does the things He does. We try to follow Him and do right by Him, but when things don't go our way, we question Him. But with God, when He closes a door to something *we* think would be great for us, it means that *He* has something much better in store for us. It's hard at times to wait for answers as to why things don't work out, but God will provide the knowledge in due time. As Paul states in Romans, God causes *everything* to work for the good of those who love and follow Him.

Not long after he got home that day, Jason received a phone call from a friend he'd had since the eighth grade. Joe, Jason's friend, asked to meet him at a local club to talk, and Jason agreed. When he arrived at the club, Jason listened to Joe's compelling story. Until recently, Joe had never been to church, owned a Bible, or recognized that God was in control. But while driving around one day, something happened that Joe couldn't understand. He felt a 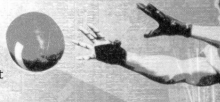 presence in his car and heard a voice telling him, "It's time, Joe, to follow Me." Joe didn't know who to turn to except his friend Jason. Jason spent the next several hours in the club sharing his faith with Joe. At two in the morning, Joe became a follower of Jesus Christ.

Why was Jason cut from the team? I don't know. But I do know that if he had made the team, he would not have been available to meet with Joe. God used Jason even during a tough time in his life to bring glory to His name. Jason was a faithful, available servant. Because Jason was cut, another person came to the throne of God and started a personal relationship with Christ.

When the bad things in life cause you to doubt, hold on. God's got something good coming your way. Make sure you are ready and available.

GO:

1. How often do you question why God does what He does?

2. How can you start waiting on God for answers in your spiritual journey?

3. Today, how can you make sure you're ready and available?

WORKOUT:

Proverbs 3:5–6
Jeremiah 29:11
1 Peter 5:6

Attacks from Within

"I became extremely angry when I heard their outcry and these complaints. After seriously considering the matter, I accused the nobles and officials, saying to them, 'Each of you is charging his countrymen interest.' So I called a large assembly against them" (Nehemiah 5:6–7 HCSB).

SET:

What's worse...being beaten by your opponent because they're better than you, or being beaten by your opponent because of internal strife within your own team? In my experience, the worst teams I've been a part of, either as an athlete or coach, were the ones with the most internal problems. Preparing for your opponent is tough enough, but trying to "right the ship" from within is a totally different animal.

As Nehemiah and his crew worked to rebuild the wall in the Old Testament, they were oppressed by outside forces. They struggled financially and started to fight, which created dissention in the ranks. It was so bad that they sold their own children into slavery. Finally Nehemiah had had enough. He put his foot down and held an "all-team" meeting. I'm sure he did most of the talking.

We all deal with internal strife within our teams, churches, families, friends— pretty much anywhere we have a group of people. Satan loves to get his foot into these areas and destroy as much as he can.

Players get jealous of playing time and attention from the coaches; church members get mad because they feel snubbed by the pastor or unheard; friends overreact when they feel neglected or misread situations.... Internal problems will always be a part of life, but they take our focus off the real goal and purpose. Nehemiah put the focus back on God and on uniting the body, and that is a good lesson for all of us to follow.

As Christians, we need to work toward unity, not division. If we say we walk with Christ, shouldn't we act like it? He handled it with grace and goodness, with kindness and compassion, and with life lessons and love. He faced internal issues with His disciples, but He always took their eyes off themselves and pointed them to the truth of the gospel.

So today, when attacks come from within, be part of the solution from the Savior. Do not become part of the problem from the prince of darkness.

GO:

1. What are the internal problems that are holding your team back?

2. What role do you need to play when these attacks arise?

3. Today, how can you be part of the solution instead of part of the problem?

WORKOUT:

2 Chronicles 30:12
Psalm 133:1
1 Peter 5:8

I Should
Have Listened

"I didn't obey my teachers or listen closely to my mentors"
(Proverbs 5:13 HCSB).

SET:

"It's okay. They won't hurt you...." "It will make you better,
bigger, stronger...." "Don't worry, no one will ever know...." These
are some of the phrases that student athletes hear when they
are encouraged to take steroids. The pursuit of greatness is so
powerful today that many athletes—young athletes—are doing
things that put their lives in jeopardy. I am sure there are two
voices they are hearing, but there is only one they should be
listening to.

Proverbs 5 addresses the topic of staying away from things
that are bad for you. In this passage, the example is immoral
women, but these instructions relate to every area of our lives.
In verse 13, we hear the remorse of someone who wished they
would have listened to the wise advice they received instead of
choosing to follow the crowd or their own evil desires. But this
still rings true in sports and society in the present day.

Today, athletes are getting wise counsel from
coaches, trainers, parents, and pastors, but
they are also getting advice from those
who do not have their best interests
at heart. Whether the struggle is
with steroids, drugs, drinking,
pornography, or something
else, athletes must choose to

listen to wise advice. It is crucial! Their minds often want to choose the immediate over the long-term, but it is the eternal, not the internal, that really matters. Coaches who push athletes to take steroids so they can win more games are beyond foolish. Athletes who push their teammates to do things that will ultimately hurt them are not true teammates.

Listen only to those who truly want what is best for you athletically, socially, academically, and most importantly, spiritually. Don't be the one to say, "I should have listened." By then it will be too late!

GO:

1. When is it difficult for you to listen to the right voices?

2. Have you been guilty of doing wrong things in trying to be a better athlete?

3. How can you start today to listen to the right voices in your life?

WORKOUT:

Proverbs 5
James 1:19

What Are You Looking For?

"The one who searches for what is good finds favor, but if someone looks for trouble, it will come to him" (Proverbs 11:27 HCSB).

Have you ever heard the old saying, "Whatever you're looking for, you're bound to find it"? It sure rings true today. And the trouble is that many people are searching in all the wrong places for all the wrong things.

What about you? What are you looking for? Are you looking for the good things in life? Proverbs 11 teaches that if we look for good, then good things are bound to happen. But if we look for bad or evil things, watch out...we will probably find what we're looking for. What about when dealing with your friends and others? Do you look for the good in them, or are you looking for something bad to use against them? Just remember that what you find you will have to deal with as well.

I know a man who sees the good in everyone. He may not care for everyone, but he always looks past the bad to see the good. What a great trait to have! It's important to seek the good in everything: spiritual truth, scripture memorization, eternal memories with loved ones, and so on. But too many times we seek the immediate, quick fixes that take us down the wrong roads. One way to always find the good, however, is to keep Jesus first! When He is in control, the good rises to the surface. When we resist Him, bad things are bound to happen. So, today, choose Jesus and the good that comes with Him!

GO:

1. What are you searching for?

2. How can you find the good in life and in others?

3. How does Jesus help us to look for the good and put off the bad?

WORKOUT:

Psalm 34:10–14
Psalm 122:9
Proverbs 11
1 Peter 3:11

What's in Your Wallet?

" 'Don't collect for yourselves treasures on earth, where moth and rust destroy and where thieves break in and steal. But collect for yourselves treasures in heaven, where neither moth nor rust destroys, and where thieves don't break in and steal. For where your treasure is, there your heart will be also' " (Matthew 6:19–21 HCSB).

SET:

"Why do you want to make it to the NFL?" This was a question I recently posed to three promising athletes. The first responded with an expected answer. He wanted the glory, fame, and money that came with being an NFL athlete. He wanted to be rich. The second player wanted to fulfill a dream of playing at the highest level and to help his family. The third player took time to think before answering.

A popular credit card commercial asks this question: "What's in your wallet?" For me, usually a couple of pictures of my family and not much more. Many others, however, live their lives to fill their earthly wallets. They want to buy all the things that will give them earthly pleasure and success. But while their wallets and bank accounts are overflowing and full, their spiritual wallets are bankrupt or depleting fast.

Is wanting money and wealth a bad thing? No—unless that's where you put your heart! Jesus instructed us not to build up treasures here on earth, but to store up treasures in heaven. Worldly wealth will pass away, but heavenly hearts are eternal.

The third player finally answered my question. He wanted to be good enough to make it into the league so that he could earn enough money to make a difference in his community for Christ. This was a young man with a heavenly heart who desired to please his Father above. Again, there is nothing wrong with having fame and fortune, but what you do with it will tell where your heart and treasure truly are. Today, if your wallet is overflowing, in whose kingdom are you making a difference? Yours or God's?

GO:

1. Where are you storing up treasures?

2. Does your wealth make an eternal difference, or just a personal one?

3. Today, how can you start to better your service to the Lord by giving of your time, talents, and treasures?

WORKOUT:

Matthew 6:19–24
Proverbs 15:16

LaDainian Tomlinson sits peacefully in a cushy interview chair in the San Diego Chargers' draft room. His schedule is busy, but he waits patiently to be miked up and enjoys the break his legs are getting after the team's morning workout. The silent attitude of his heart is communicated to those in the room by the grin on his face. He's happy, and it shows.

"Of course he's happy," you think. "He's one of the best running backs in the NFL, and he makes millions of dollars."

Well, yeah.

LT is happy because he's been blessed with athletic talent and money to spare. He knows that the more he has, the more he can give away. And nothing makes him happier than to bless others out of his abundance.

One of LT's favorite verses is Luke 12:48: "Much will be required of everyone who has been given much" (HCSB). The passage, which is a direct quote from Jesus to His disciples, is one LT's mother instilled in him when he was young and now serves as one of his core life principles. It sits there in the back of his mind, waiting to be recalled during any moment that he

might need to explain just why he is so generous with his time
and resources.

Many who read Luke 12:48 are overwhelmed by the
responsibility it commands, but not LT. He wants to be a
role model. He's had that desire since he was in high school.
He wanted the Lord to call him to a high position so that he
could positively impact student athletes the same way he was
influenced at that age.

He got his wish. Now one of the most influential men in
sports, LT is thriving on his ability to bless those in need.

Here is a portion of an interview with LT on how he gets
"One Day Better" as a cheerful giver. The entire article was
published in November 2008 in FCA's "Sharing the Victory"
magazine.

***Second Corinthians 9:7 says that the Lord loves a cheerful
giver. Is that you?***
LT: Most definitely. I've always been that way, and that really
comes from my family. I was raised in a family of givers. That's
just our belief in our calling and in what we should be doing
by helping others.

Why do you focus so much on giving to and serving others?
LT: It's kind of hard to explain, but I think it comes from
seeing the joy on people's faces when you give them
something. That gift is something they will always remember,
whether it's big or small. That's what I get the most joy from,
because I remember the time when I was the one who needed

a handout and someone did it for me. I remember how I felt in receiving that gift.

How does your faith in Christ motivate you to give?
LT: I think Christ living in me helps me to do that. It's something I don't even have to think about, to be honest with you. I don't struggle with it; it's just automatic. Something inside of me says, "Give. Okay, you can give a little more. Now do a little more. You can help this person." That's how it works for me.

With your passion for young people, if you could have the attention of every student athlete in the country for five minutes, what would you say to them?
LT: I would probably tell them this: If you fly into a city where you've never been, you're going to need directions—something to tell you where to go in that city because you've never been there before. If you don't have directions, you're going to get lost.

For me, that's the way Christ is in my life. Without Him, I'm lost. I don't have any direction. I don't know which way I'm heading.

I would tell them that you have to have some direction in life. You have to know the foundation of your life and where you're going in order to be successful.

Now, are we going to mess up? Yes, it happens. But the whole point is getting back on track and making sure you stay focused and on the straight and narrow.

GIVING

How do you do that? How do you personally stay focused on Christ?
LT: It's all about your priorities. That's something we talk about all the time here. It's faith, family, football. Remembering to keep faith first, then family, and then football.

Tomlinson gives us a great example of how to live "One Day Better" as a person who loves to give. What can you do today to become a cheerful giver of your time, talents, and treasure for God's glory, as well? You will be glad you did!

One of the greatest running backs in the history of the NFL, LaDainian Tomlinson continues to be a force for Christ in his community. As a San Diego Charger, he holds many offensive records for his team. He is considered to be one of the most humble professional athletes in sports today.

Attitude of Gratitude

"Give thanks to the LORD, for He is good. His love is eternal" (Psalm 136:1 HCSB).

Athletes of all levels seem to feel a sense of entitlement. I have sensed over the years that there is a lack of gratefulness in them. I watch as a manager serves water to an athlete, who, in response, drops his water bottle on the ground instead of handing it back to the manager standing beside him. I see little league players get instructions from coaches, umpires, and others, only to disregard them because they think they know better. What has happened to the attitude of gratitude—of having a thankful heart for the people who serve or care enough to help?

In Psalm 136, the author wants to make a very clear point. He says twenty-six times that we should be giving thanks to the Lord. The trouble is that today we treat the Lord the same way some athletes treat those who try to help them. The Lord sends someone to encourage us, and we basically ignore their kind words. The Lord blesses us with an abundance of things, and yet we complain that we have too much stuff and clutter in our lives. All we have to do is look around.... What is there *not* to be grateful for?

The next time you see someone whose attitude is less than grateful, remind them of all we should be thankful for. The only thing we are entitled to do is give daily thanks to the Lord. Without His faithfulness, we would be lost forever. It may sound like I'm being critical here, but I'm not. I've just realized that we need to be thankful for what God has done for us. Thank You, Lord!

GO:

1. When have you experienced feelings of gratitude or entitlement?

2. What do you need to thank the Lord for?

3. How can you realize God's faithful love in your life today?

WORKOUT:

Psalm 148
Romans 5:8–11
Ephesians 1:6–8

Talk Is Cheap

READY:

"To the pure, everything is pure, but to those who are defiled and unbelieving nothing is pure; in fact, both their mind and conscience are defiled. They profess to know God, but they deny Him by their works. They are detestable, disobedient, and disqualified for any good work" (Titus 1:15–16 HCSB).

SET:

I had many favorite sayings as a coach. Here are some of them:

- Rule 1: The coach is right. Rule 2: If you think Coach is wrong, see Rule 1.
- Whether you can or can't, you are right.
- Don't tell me. Show me.

The last one may have been my favorite. Athletes have a hard time backing up what they say. They talk a good game, but many times today's athletes can't show it by their actions. All in all, talk is cheap.

In the book of Titus, Paul encouraged true believers to stand strong. Many people in that time were all talk and didn't live up to their words, especially when it came to Christ. Paul called these kinds of people despicable, disobedient, and worthless for doing anything good. Wow. Tough words, huh?

In James, we find a simple message: Do not just talk or listen to the Word, but be doers of it (James 1). Christ said that if you are going to tell Him you love Him, also show

Him. Peter was a prime example of cheap talk. His heart was good, but he did not always walk his talk and did not consistently show Christ that his talk was a reflection of his true belief.

All coaches want to believe that their players will do what they say all the time, but they know that that's not always the case. If your coach can convince your team to talk less and do more, you are likely to find a greater level of success in your sport. Jesus wants the same for His believers. He wants us to talk less about all the great things we intend to do for Him and just start doing them. He wants a lifestyle of action, not one of mere talk. Athletes and Christians need to heed the same message: Talk is cheap, and action is everything.

GO:

1. Are you normally a talker or a doer? When have you been a doer?

2. In your life, where do you find that you are a cheap talker?

3. Today, how can you show Christ that you want to keep Him first in all you do?

WORKOUT:

James 1:22–25
James 2:14–26
1 John 3:18–20

Be a David

"David said to Saul, 'Don't let anyone be discouraged by him; your servant will go and fight this Philistine!' " (1 Samuel 17:32 HCSB).

SET:

Competitive toughness is something all athletes strive for. Tennis legend Chris Evert once said, "Competitive toughness is an acquired skill, not an inherited gift." The ability to be mentally and physically tough in sports today is something that athletes have to work for daily. Just because your parents may have been great athletes does not mean you will be. You have to work on it.

The Bible's David developed competitive toughness as a young boy. He watched the family's flock of sheep, fended off lions and bears, and endured a long stretch of patience when he wanted to fight in battle but was not allowed. When David finally got his chance, however, he was ready. He willingly took on a massive warrior and won. He was not afraid of Goliath because he knew he could defeat him. The Lord was with David, and David had that edge to help him throughout the rest of his life.

As the described "man after God's own heart," David's example can teach us many things from both in and beyond his bout with Goliath. In fact, we should all be Davids when it comes to certain areas:

1. Courageously defend your flock against the lions and bears of the world.

2. Be willing to fight the Goliaths in life, one stone at a time.

3. Be a loyal friend no matter what the situation.
4. Be ready to lead, regardless of your age or status.
5. Face your failures and own up to them.
6. Never take forgiveness lightly or a blessing for granted.
7. Learn from your mistakes.
8. Strive to develop trust and faith in your teammates.
9. Create an unchangeable belief in God's faithfulness.
10. Chase success, but pursue God's heart.

We can learn a lot from David's successes and failures, and I would encourage you to read about his entire life when you have the time so that you can fully understand each point on the list above. However, in the end, we can summarize "being a David" by loving God, loving others, and loving life. Be tough, be competitive, be a Christian in the midst of the battle, and be a David—a man after God's own heart.

GO:

1. When do you feel tough in your sport?

2. In what spiritual areas do you need to get tougher?

3. How can you be a David in the midst of life's daily grind?

WORKOUT:

1 Samuel 17
1 Timothy 6:12
1 Timothy 4:7

Off-Season Workout

"The son who gathers during summer is prudent; the son who sleeps during harvest is disgraceful" (Proverbs 10:5 HCSB).

SET:

When I was a coach, one of the hardest things I dealt with was getting my athletes to understand that improvement took place in the off-season. I would always get the same song and dance about their working hard during the season and needing the time off. Let me tell you something. Work ethic is a big deal to a coach. Athletes who put in the work are always better off in the end.

In Proverbs 10, Solomon teaches us about a wise young man. He worked hard all summer and did not waste time being lazy or playing too many video games. Okay, that's my version of the story. But the young people in Solomon's day made the most of their time and efforts. There are so many distractions now that it is difficult to get young athletes to understand that improvement in a sport takes year-round effort. It does my heart good to drive home from work and see young people shooting baskets, playing catch, jogging, or even riding bikes. At least they are doing something other than sitting inside all day and loafing around. (I hear a collective "Amen" from the parents out there.)

Solomon did not say that hard work was a 24/7 thing, but it does take effort. Whatever your work may be—a summer job or your sport—*work* at it. Spend time working on the things you struggle with as an athlete so that when next season rolls around, you will be able to show your coaches that your summer was not wasted.

This concept also applies to our walk with Christ. We must constantly strive to grow closer to Him. We must spend time in getting to know Him better, not waste our time on other useless pursuits. I heard a promising high school quarterback say recently, "If kids our age would spend as much time reading the Bible as they do on video games, what kind of world would we have today?" Interesting thought. Now what will you do about it?

GO:

1. What does your summer workout routine look like?

2. Are you content with where you are at as an athlete? As a Christian?

3. Today, how can you start working hard for Christ's glory?

WORKOUT:

Proverbs 10
Matthew 25:14–30
Colossians 3:23–24
Hebrews 6:10–12

S.D.M.S.

"Peter replied, 'Even if all fall away on account of you, I never will' " (Matthew 26:33 NIV).

SET:

Recently I was diagnosed with a serious condition. This condition can affect every part of life—and can be fatal if not taken care of quickly. It is called S.D.M.S.—Stubborn Dumb Male Syndrome. I have had it for some time but only recently realized how bad my condition had gotten. In fact, many men have this condition. It can strike at any time and any place—on the field or off the field, at home, at school, or even in church. If not treated, it can harden a man's heart and turn him from the proper remedy.

One man found in scripture who probably had this condition was known as the "rock." Peter was definitely a candidate for S.D.M.S. How many times do we find Peter acting impulsively or stubbornly to prove his point or faith in Christ? Recall the water-walking incident...or the time when Peter had the guard lend him an ear—literally. But the classic occasion occurred when Peter displayed his stubborn will by telling Christ that he would never do such a thing as deny Him. Well, as the story goes, Peter failed again and denied his Savior not once but three times. Peter always meant well, but his S.D.M.S. condition often held him back. Thank goodness (and thank God) for forgiveness!

Why do many of us have this condition? We suffer from thinking that we know more than others, and we even put our will before God's. However,

106

this condition can be cured or
helped with the proper medicine,
which comes in several forms:
a dose of prayer, reading God's
Word, swallowing one's pride, and
asking for forgiveness and grace. When I realized that my
condition was worsening, I went to get healing—healing from
the Great Physician. He can cure you and restore you to proper
spiritual health.

S.D.M.S. may never been fully cured, but it can be controlled!
Just remember that God's faithfulness can compensate for our
greatest failures in mind, body, and spirit.

GO:

1. How much do you suffer from S.D.M.S.?

2. What areas of your life does this condition affect the most?

3. Today, will you begin faithfully taking the proper
medication for the condition?

WORKOUT:

Romans 12:2
Ephesians 4:22–24
1 Corinthians 1:25

Didn't See
It Coming

"Then the LORD opened the donkey's mouth...." (Numbers 22:28 NIV).

SET:

Mike was a great miler. He always liked to take the lead early in the race and run to victory. His coach, however, was concerned about an upcoming race. Mike's top opponent was one who liked to come from behind to win.

When the event started, Mike raced to the lead like clockwork. His coach told him to move to the inside of lane one, but Mike ignored him. He liked to run in the first lane, but not always on the inside. On laps two and three his coach said the same thing, and Mike grew upset with him. Mike knew he had the lead—the victory was his. On lap four, his coach became more insistent that Mike move to the inside of the lane, but Mike stayed firm in the middle.

In the Old Testament, Balaam had a similar situation with his faithful donkey. Balaam was traveling down the road on his donkey, but God sent an angel to oppose Balaam, as He was angry with him. The donkey could see the angel, although Balaam could not. The donkey moved to avoid the angel, and Balaam became angry and hit his donkey. Three times the donkey avoided the angel, who was sent to strike down Balaam, and Balaam hit his faithful steed every time. Finally God opened the donkey's mouth, and she and Balaam had a conversation. Now, if my donkey started talking to me, I'd certainly take notice, but Balaam was so blinded by his anger that he did not listen. God had to open Balaam's eyes to see what the donkey had saved him from receiving. Balaam repented of his sin and turned to God for forgiveness.

On the final turn of his race, Mike stayed firmly in his chosen position. In the last ten yards, his opponent passed him on the inside and took the victory. Mike's coach had seen what Mike himself could not. He knew Mike's opponent was coming on strong and that if Mike did not move to the inside, he would be beaten. Mike, like Balaam, had a blind spot and could not see what was coming.

Many times we do not listen to others who want to show us areas of improvement because we cannot see the need ourselves. We all have blind spots. But pay attention. God may be using others to show you what you need to change today.

GO:

1. What are the blind spots in your life as an athlete and a Christian?

2. Who has helped you to see your blind spots?

3. How can you eliminate your spiritual blind spots?

WORKOUT:

Proverbs 12:15
Proverbs 13:10
Proverbs 15:22

In Pursuit Of...

"But just as he who called you is holy, so be holy in all you do; for it is written: 'Be holy, because I am holy' " (1 Peter 1:15–16 NIV).

Grades, money, sports, championships...the list goes on and on. These are the things we are in constant pursuit of these days. On the surface these things are not inherently bad, but are we consumed by these pursuits? I see nothing wrong with wanting good grades or to excel in sports or to ultimately win a championship during a season, but those should not be our end-all pursuits.

I have been reading an old book I got from my brother Jim for my high school graduation. I read it then, but it had very little impact on my life until I picked it up some twenty-four years later. Jerry Bridges's book, *The Pursuit of Holiness,* has rekindled the light that had gone dim over these past years. One of my favorite quotes from the book is, "God does not require a perfect, sinless life to have fellowship with Him, but He does require that we be serious about holiness, that we grieve over sin in our lives instead of justifying it, and that we earnestly pursue holiness as a way of life." Like the old Batman shows, I got a *bam, smack, pow,* right upside my head to wake me up as to what I need to be pursuing in my life.

As an athlete, what are you pursuing outside of your sporting life? Too many times we become defeated by sin and then justify it because of some life crisis we might be going through, but that just doesn't cut it by His standard. Our problem in life is that we are living by the world's standards, not God's. God's standard is pretty simple: " 'Be holy, because I am holy' " (1 Peter 1:16 NIV). We are to pursue holiness in our lives. Okay, so it doesn't sound as glamorous as pursuing a third championship ring or the newest Hummer on the lot, but those things won't get you any closer to God. You can pursue anything in life, but the only pursuit that will make an eternal difference is your pursuit of holiness. Remember, God has called every Christian to a holy life; there is no getting around it, no matter how hard you try.

GO:

1. What are some evidences of holiness in your life today?

2. Which sins bother you enough to change and seek the help God wants to give for you to become like Him?

3. What are some specific areas of your life that will change as you begin to pursue holiness?

WORKOUT:

Genesis 2:3
Matthew 7:21–23
Exodus 15:11
1 Thessalonians 4:4

The economic struggles of the United States strike Albert Pujols differently than most. After all, when you've grown up amid conditions far worse than what the average American considers difficult, it puts things in perspective. While the economic crash of the U.S. is indeed serious if not critical, the reality remains that many countries are filled with citizens who have been battling for years to find a single daily meal.

No, Pujols himself was never a starving child, but he wasn't wealthy. And the scenes he saw growing up in the Dominican Republic, where he lived before moving with his family to the U.S. at the age of fifteen, have fueled in him a passion for reaching those in need.

As one of the most prolific sluggers in modern-day baseball, Pujols is able to use his fame to capitalize on his desire to reach out. Each year, through his Pujols Family Foundation, he and his wife, Deidre, along with a team of staff and volunteers, lead medical mission trips to the Dominican Republic. Through these trips, they have brought teams of dentists and eye doctors to the Caribbean country.

In 2008, Major League Baseball recognized Pujols's efforts

by giving him the Roberto Clemente Award, the highest honor a player can receive for his efforts in the community.

While the awards are nice (especially one named after the legendary Clemente), Pujols would maintain his mission with or without recognition. After all, it's not just about being a "nice guy" or a positive role model. It's about fulfilling a calling he's been given straight from his Lord.

The following is a portion of an interview that FCA's "Sharing the Victory" had with Albert Pujols and published in April 2009.

As the winner of last season's Roberto Clemente Award, you obviously have a passion for community outreach. How is that an extension of your faith in Christ?

Albert Pujols: Well, I think that's our main goal: to try to reach people not just through our foundation or through writing a check but with the good news of Jesus Christ. We want to make sure that we do that in the community here as well as in the Dominican Republic. I think that's our main job.

People sometimes ask me, "What is your job?" Everybody thinks that it's playing baseball, but that's not my job; that's the platform God has given me. My job is to be obedient to Him and do the things He wants me to do for His will, not for Albert Pujols. And when I talk to somebody who's a Christian and believes what I believe, they understand. But other people can't understand, and I want to make sure I explain it to them and share with them what God has done in my life.

GET REAL WITH GOD

How did you first come to faith in Christ?

AP: When I met my wife as an eighteen-year-old in 1998, we started going to church. Down in the Dominican, I'd had the opportunity to go to church, but I didn't realize that Jesus Christ really wanted a personal relationship with me. When I was in the Dominican, all I cared about was my education and playing baseball. It's not that I didn't care about going to church, but that wasn't my passion. That wasn't what I was looking for. What I was looking for was to be a professional athlete.

When I came to the United States, I found out that it was more than just a religion. God wanted a personal relationship with me. On November 13, 1998, I started going to church with my wife, and by the second week I gave my life to Christ.

Obviously I was a baby in Christ, and I had to mature a lot. And it wasn't until June 2000 that God started moving in my life. Until that point, my wife and I had been living a sinful life. We weren't married, but we were living together.

So I think God wasn't moving in us until we decided to get married and live our lives right. But that's how I gave my life to the Lord, and obviously since then it's been being renewed. I wish I could have made that decision or opened my eyes sooner and found out about that relationship, but I believe that God has a plan for everybody, and that was His plan for me.

The mission statement of your foundation is "Faith, Family, Others." Can you explain why it's in that order?

AP: Well, first is faith; it's about Jesus Christ. Then, what is the second-most important thing after Jesus Christ? Your family.

Then, lastly, it is making sure that we share the good news with others. That is why we put it in that order.

At the same time, we want to stay humble, knowing that it's not about us; it's about God. The Pujols Family Foundation isn't about Albert Pujols; it's about Jesus Christ. We want to make sure that we don't lose that edge and that focus of what we're here to do.

One purpose of your foundation is to provide aid to those who are living in impoverished conditions in the Dominican Republic. You've been in the U.S. for a long time, but you obviously still have a passion for where you spent your childhood. Tell me why that is on your heart.

AP: Well, I left when I was fifteen years old, but I kind of grew up in those conditions. I know what kind of tough conditions are there.

When we go down there, we are going to touch a lot of lives, but we can't touch the lives of all nine or ten million people who live in the Dominican Republic. But what we can do is make an example for others to follow. And I think the Lord has blessed me with the ability to play sports and given me the platform—and He could have chosen anyone else, but He decided to choose me. So I want to make sure that I do His will and do it the right way.

I grew up poor, but I have love, and I have a family. Some of these kids who are poor may not even know what love means. Their mom and dad may be divorced, or they might have been abused by their parents. I know there are a lot of tough situations, just like here in the United States. But it's a little different because it is a poor country.

So I try to make sure I never forget where I came from and about those people, because there is a need, and it is all over the place—all over the globe. And we as Christians have to make sure that we don't forget that there's a need out there.

Right now, the U.S. is going through some tough economic challenges. While those are very real, the fact is that there are places in far more impoverished situations. Do you ever find it difficult to listen to people talk about their wealth problems when you've seen conditions that are so much worse?

AP: I think sometimes our focus gets centered on us instead of on Jesus, and we forget that we have to thank God for what we have. And I'm guilty of that. Sometimes I'm like, "God, forgive me, because that person probably wishes he was in the situation that I'm in right now." I complain when He has given me everything I need. And the most important thing He's given me is eternal life, which you can't buy.

But I think, as Americans, we may not have a job or are struggling with money, but we forget that there are people out there who go days without even eating. And that's their life. They've been living like that for fifteen to twenty years. I think we tend to forget about the people in other countries who are struggling worse than we are.

My kid is eight years old, and I try to explain to him where everything comes from. I think that sometimes our teenagers, because their parents can't afford to give them that new pair of shoes or whatever they want at that moment, will complain and be miserable. But down there in the Dominican, they don't have that. I always suggest to parents that they take their kids, as soon as they turn fifteen or sixteen, on a mission trip so that they can see how blessed they are by what they have here in the United States compared to the situations of some of the kids in other countries.

How have those mission trips changed you personally?
AP: They've changed me a lot. Obviously I grew up in a tougher place—not exactly like those people, but I have gone through some tough things in my life. And every time I go down there I'm grateful, and I thank God for what I've got and for everything that He provides me every day. I thank Him just for giving me the opportunity to come here to the United States to reach my goal of becoming a professional athlete and to find the best thing that ever happened in my life, and that's Him.

But I think that's something I look at when I go down to the Dominican, you know? That was me. And that's what keeps me humble every day.

Albert Pujols is one of the best baseball players in this current generation. His greatness is not limited to the field only; he is a devoted husband and father whose mission is to reach others for Christ through his testimony.

The Chosen

"Therefore, God's chosen ones, holy and loved..."
(Colossians 3:12 HCSB).

SET:

Danny was not a good athlete. In fact, he was pretty bad. I remember how he always hated recess. When we were in the third grade, we played a killer game of kickball every recess, and every boy played...except for Danny. He always watched closely, though. One day the sides were uneven, and I was named captain. I knew what I had to do. With my first pick in the 1970 First Round Draft for recess kickball, I chose Danny Anderson. After everyone got up off the ground from laughing, Danny walked over to my side with his head down.

We are lucky people, don't you think? What? You don't feel lucky? You should. You have been chosen. When God looked over all the people, He chose *you*! Isn't that awesome? Why did He choose you? You are a sinner, the scum of the earth, a jerk by all standards, at times. But because of His love for you and the holiness He desires for your life—and because He knows what you are capable of doing—He chose you to be on His team forever!

In Matthew 4, we read that Jesus encouraged His disciples to "come follow Me!" He chose them, just like He chose you and me. What a great feeling to know that not only have you been chosen but that you are loved, as well. It doesn't get any better than that.

Danny came over to me and said, "Jere, what are you thinking? I'm the worst player in class." My response was simple, "You might not be as good as some of the others, but you are the best encourager I know." With that, Danny's whole expression changed. He was right. He was a bad player and made an out every time, but you never saw anyone encourage his team to victory as much as Danny did that day. For a day, Danny Anderson was chosen. With Christ, you can be chosen, as well. Have you chosen Him to be the Lord of your entire life? He chose you. Will you chose Him?

GO:

1. Have you ever been picked first? How did it feel?
2. Have you chosen to follow Christ forever?
3. Today, what can you do to start living a life as one who has been chosen by God?

WORKOUT:

Romans 8:31–39
1 Thessalonians 1:4–5
1 Peter 2:9

Run and Hide

"The son said to him, 'Father, I have sinned against heaven and against you. I am no longer worthy to be called your son' " (Luke 15:21 NIV).

SET:

De'Andre had it all: a great college basketball career behind him, a Master's degree from a prestigious institution, and an awesome job on Capitol Hill. He had the world by the tail, and he thought he had done it all on his own. Thinking he didn't need any help, he walked away from his faith and continued to thrive by the world's standards. But when the things of the world didn't fill him up, he decided that he needed more. He left his career to chase a dream. That wasn't necessarily a bad thing, as this is where his true adventure began. But when his dream crumbled, he ran and hid. People offered help, love, and care, but he was lost in the sin of the world. He had no desire to return home to Christ.

De'Andre's story is similar to the story of the prodigal son in the Bible. The son was tired of his good life. He wanted more, needed more, desired more. He asked his father for his part of the family wealth and left home to chase his dream. When the young man's dreams were proved empty and his money was gone, he was left to eat with the pigs. He was definitely down on his luck. But then this young man did a wise thing. He got up and went home. He went home, confessed his sins, and begged for forgiveness from his father. He felt unworthy, but his father didn't care about that. He loved his son too much and was just glad that he was home.

I would love to tell you that De'Andre turned back to his heavenly Father for help, but sadly he hasn't. He believes he can continue to run and hide from Him and wants nothing to do with the faith that guided him to where he was in the first place. He now has turned to a life of sin. He blames God and others for not being there in his time of need. What is the difference between the prodigal son and De'Andre? About eight inches. The son knew in his head and believed in his heart that he could always come home to his father. The father was looking and waiting for him to come home.

Are you like De'Andre? Are you trying to run and hide from God today? Stop blaming God for your circumstances and run home to Him. He is waiting and looking for you to run into His open arms of love. Only He can make all the pain of life go away. Trust Him again today!

GO:

1. How can you relate to De'Andre?

2. Are you playing hide and seek from Christ?

3. Today, what can you do to not run and hide but run and thrive with Him?

WORKOUT:

Matthew 4:17
Luke 15
1 John 1:9

Spiritual Twinkies

READY:

"Do not love this world nor the things it offers you, for when you love the world, you do not have the love of the Father in you. For the world offers only a craving for physical pleasure, a craving for everything we see, and pride in our achievements and possessions. These are not from the Father, but are from this world. And this world is fading away...." (1 John 2:15–17 NLT).

SET:

Athletes today need the best foods to nourish their bodies for maximum performance, but every once in a while we all eat things that are not good for us. One of those snack foods that trip up many a person is the dreaded Twinkie. Did you know that over 500 million Twinkies are sold each year? That's a lot of consumed junk food. I've actually have never eaten a Twinkie, but many an Oreo has crossed my path. Now, occasional junk food is not entirely bad for us, but many times one such temptation is not enough; we continue to go back for more until we can't stop. Most people have the self-control to stop, but some cannot, and they develop a problem.

When the disciple John wrote the letter of 1 John, he talked about those who cannot stop loving the world. The world today is like a big Twinkie. Sure, it looks good...might even taste good...but it has no spiritual nutritional value for you. In my Monday morning small group, one of the men labeled the things of this world as "spiritual Twinkies"— things like most TV shows, movies, music, internet, alcohol, and on and on. Anything this world offers that has no spiritual nourishment or redeeming value, in my mind, would be considered a spiritual Twinkie.

In our verses today we see that everything on this earth is fading away. However, those who want to live their lives doing God's will can live forever with Him (see the end of verse 17). The so-called "spiritual Twinkies" can rob us from truly living for Christ. Too much of this world will only lead someone away from their ultimate goal of heaven, just as too much junk food can hinder the path of a finely tuned athlete.

I am not telling you to go throw away all your junk food, but God's Word does command us to rid ourselves of anything that keeps us from being fully devoted to Him. So, essentially, get rid of those spiritual Twinkies that are weighing you down!

GO:

1. What are you indulging in today?

2. What spiritual Twinkies are weighing you down?

3. This week, how can you be in the world but not of it?

WORKOUT:

Hebrews 12:1–2
1 Corinthians 10:13
Galatians 5:19–25

The Only Name You Need

" 'You will conceive and give birth to a son, and you will name him Jesus' " (Luke 1:31 NLT).

Recently I saw an interview where Magic Johnson was talking with LeBron James about his success in the league. The conversation turned to former players who did so well they were known by one name or nickname—athletes like MJ, Tiger, Junior, Kobe, Sweetness, Shaq, Magic, Dr. J, and now LeBron. James said he was honored to be put in such high athletic royalty with these other men, and he hoped he would be around to see the next "one-named" guy come on the scene.

God's Word is filled with one-named guys—Moses, Noah, Joseph, Daniel, and others—but there is one name that stands above all other names. At this name, every knee will bow and every tongue will confess that *He* is Lord. In His name, people were healed, the possessed became whole, and lives were changed. Men and women throughout history have endangered and given up their lives for this name's sake. All things were created by Him and for Him. And it all began through a young girl chosen to bear a son and call Him the name above all names...Jesus. All those great athletes in history who attained "one-named" status never came close to what the greatest name on earth achieved for us. It is in His name we

124

pray. You don't hear anyone pray,
"Kobe, in your name we pray...."
No other name fits but the name
of Jesus. So as you recognize these
great athletes by their one-name
monikers, let's not forget that the only name you will ever
need to remember is that of *Jesus*. Honor the others, but serve
the greatest Name of all!

GO:

1. Who are some other athletes or people you can think of
who have been given "one-named" status?

2. When you hear the name *Jesus*, what comes to your mind
and heart?

3. How can you serve the "Name above all names" better
today?

WORKOUT:

Acts 15:25–27
Ephesians 5:15–20
Acts 3:1–16

Just Do It

"Do not merely listen to the word, and so deceive yourselves. Do what it says" (James 1:22 NIV).

SET:

How many times do we see it? A coach is instructing his players in how to do a certain task. They hear what the coach says, but they go out and do just the opposite. Where did the lines get crossed? Where was the breakdown in communication? Bottom line—why didn't they do what the coach wanted them to do?

The answer can be complex, but it's also pretty simple. They *heard* what the coach said but were not *listening* to what to do. They forgot to apply what was needed to accomplish their task at hand.

How many times are we guilty of that spiritually? James reminds us not to just listen to the Word, but to do it. Maybe James should get some Nike commission for the old ad "Just Do It," but the concept still rings true today as we need to apply sound scriptural teachings into our everyday life.

As a coach, I always loved seeing our game plan come together and work because my players applied what they had been taught. I am sure God is pleased the same way. When we apply His commands in our lives, His game plan for us always seems to be right on track!

Let's not be spiritual players who only listen on Sunday; instead, let's be ones who take God's Word and "Just Do It"!

126

GO:

1. Are you simply hearing the Word, or are you really listening to what He is teaching you?

2. How can you put God's Word into action in your life?

3. Are you willing to "Just Do It" for Him?

WORKOUT:

James 1:22

Running on the Edge

"Mark out a straight path for your feet; stay on the safe path" (Proverbs 4:26 NLT).

SET:

Driving down the road recently, I saw something that made me take notice. Coming toward me was a middle-aged man running against the traffic. Now, that did not bother me so much; I see that all the time. But what I found strange was that he had on his iPod and was running right along the edge of the cars. Not ten feet from him on his left was a beautiful, well-groomed sidewalk, on which there was not a single person. I couldn't help but break out into laughter.

After I stopped laughing, God spoke to me. "What's so funny?" I felt Him asking. "You do that all the time." I respectfully replied, "I do not. I don't even run anymore." Okay, it's probably not a great idea to get sarcastic with the Creator of the world. I knew where He was going. He reminded me of the sin in my life and how many times I run, walk, and live on the edge of sin when He (the Creator of the perfect path) has given me a clear and safe sidewalk.

Why is it that we, like this iPoded man, run in harm's way on the edge of sin? Maybe we think we can stay on the edge and never go over it. But Satan, the creator of all sin, does not play fair, and he will do anything he can to bring us to the brink of destruction.

Proverbs 4:26 tells us to mark out a straight path for our feet and stay on the safe path—the path God intends for us.

What does "running on the edge" mean to you? Maybe it is the party everyone goes to after the game, being alone with your girlfriend, or staying up late and watching something questionable on TV. I don't know what the edge is for you, but you do! Running on the sidewalk of life may not be appealing, but it is the safest place to be. God provides us with a safe path. Our job is to run, walk, and live in it.

GO:

1. When was the last time you were running on life's edge?

2. What are those areas in your life that tend to drag you to the edge?

3. How can you run, walk, and live on the safe path with Christ daily?

WORKOUT:

Psalm 1:6
Proverbs 4:27
1 Corinthians 10:13

Practice, Practice, Practice

"Proclaim the message; persist in it whether convenient or not; rebuke, correct, and encourage with great patience and teaching" (2 Timothy 4:2 HCSB).

I love to golf. I used to be fairly good. Well, kind of good. Okay, just average. But I love to play! The thing I don't like about golf is practicing. Hitting a couple of putts, swinging the club to loosen up, and then going out to play has been my golf routine in recent years. So why should I expect to be any good? Getting better at something takes practice, practice, and more practice. Golf is no exception. No wonder Tiger and Vijay are so good!

One thing Paul understood about sharing his faith was that it took practice, and lots of it! He was always ready to practice sharing his faith with someone. And Paul passed on his practice of sharing to Timothy. He instructed Timothy to be ready to share his faith at all times. Practicing sharing our faith should be a privilege we look forward to instead of a torturous experience. And when we do share our faith, we need to make sure we know the details. Part of our practice time needs to be spent in studying God's Word to know what it says. God's Word always supersedes man's word.

As much as I love golf, I will never improve without consistent practice. As we grow in Christ, sharing our faith will require

130

more practice, too. The more we share our faith, the easier it will become. In the end, no matter how much I improve at golf, it doesn't measure up to the practice of sharing my faith with others. Today, start making it a daily habit to share about Christ. All that practice will pay off in the end.

GO:

1. How do you feel about practicing your sport? Your faith?

2. When was the last time you shared your faith?

3. How can you begin the practice of sharing your faith with unbelievers?

WORKOUT:

Acts 6:4
1 Thessalonians 2:13
1 Peter 1:25

GET REAL WITH GOD

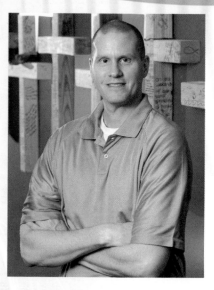

After one of my recent speaking engagements, a gentleman came up to chat. He told me that he worked in a kind of undercover capacity. I was intrigued and started asking him questions. Well, of course he couldn't tell me too much! However, he said that when he does undercover work, he has to have some type of "cover" so people won't know what he is really doing. He told me that he chose to be an open-air preacher and hand out tracts as his "cover"! I stood there almost stunned. I said, "You get paid every day to preach the gospel and hand tracts out, but that really isn't your job?" I loved it. What a fantastic idea. I asked him how he got away with that as a "cover." He told me that he was the boss and he could make that decision! He's my kind of boss!

The whole conversation really got me thinking. Many of us do just the opposite. We are salesmen who happen to be Christians.... We are parents whose faith is only seen on Sundays.... We are plumbers, but our customers never know that we read the Bible.... We are politicians, but we don't want to mix our faith with our job.... We are teachers, but we leave

SHARING
YOUR FAITH
BY MARK CAHILL

our Christianity at the front door with the metal detector....
We are students who don't think we need to speak up against
the false teachings being propagated on college campuses....
We are keeping the most important part of ourselves—our
relationship with the almighty God—to ourselves. So even
though this world is in desperate need of eternal truth, we
rationalize that it is okay to be scared or ashamed and think
that it is not really our job to tell them people anyway. Wrong!

Once while I was still teaching, I had to hire someone to
speak at an athletic banquet. It was a Christian school, and
we wanted someone with a strong testimony to challenge
the students and parents to boldly stand for Jesus Christ.
So I hired an ex-Major League Baseball player and asked him
what he was doing for a living. He told me that he worked for
a cable company and installed cable TV in people's homes. I
asked why he did that. I thought that every ex–pro athlete
should be rolling in the dough. And, of course, reality is very
different from our perception. He looked at me and said, "The
reason I install cable TV is to get into more people's homes so
I can tell them the truth about eternity and the truth about
the crucified Savior of the world." I can't even begin to tell you
the feeling I had when this man told me his story. It was one
of the most humbling moments of my entire life. This man
had life figured out. It isn't that you go lay cable to feed the
family and pay the bills, but that you go into people's homes
to plant seeds for the Lord Jesus Christ and God allows you to
get a paycheck at the same time.

GET REAL WITH GOD

Read what is written in chapter 26 of the book of Acts, verses 23–29, in the King James Version:

"That Christ should suffer, and that he should be the first that should rise from the dead, and should shew light unto the people, and to the Gentiles. And as he thus spake for himself, Festus said with a loud voice, Paul, thou art beside thyself; much learning doth make thee mad. But he said, I am not mad, most noble Festus; but speak forth the words of truth and soberness. For the king knoweth of these things, before whom also I speak freely: for I am persuaded that none of these things are hidden from him; for this thing was not done in a corner. King Agrippa, believest thou the prophets? I know that thou believest. Then Agrippa said unto Paul, Almost thou persuadest me to be a Christian. And Paul said, I would to God, that not only thou, but also all that hear me this day, were both almost, and altogether such as I am, except these bonds."

You see, Paul wasn't standing before Festus and King Agrippa as a tentmaker. He was standing there as a man of God who happened to make tents on the side. He didn't get arrested for being a tentmaker. His real profession was making sure that Festus and King Agrippa knew the truth about Jesus Christ, period. Paul made some very powerful and direct statements to the king. He didn't worry about the consequences; he worried about being faithful to God and nothing else.

SHARING
YOUR FAITH
BY MARK CAHILL

I want to encourage you not to be an undercover Christian in the coming days. Make sure it is the part about you that most people know first and foremost. Oh, by the way, the person who was undercover told me that one day he got the chance to hand a tract to the terrorist that he had been following! He knew that jail doesn't change a man's heart, but the gospel does. Make sure no one around you will ever mistake you as an undercover Christian. Be bold!

Mark Cahill is a nationally known evangelist who is not afraid to go where others might not. A former college basketball player, he uses his talents and gifts to reach countless people for Christ. Mark travels the country teaching young people how to share their faith.

The Most Important Thing

"But you will receive power when the Holy Spirit has come upon you, and you will be My witnesses in Jerusalem, in all Judea and Samaria, and to the ends of the earth" (Acts 1:8 HCSB).

SET:

There are so many important things to do before we get to heaven: get an education, stay fit and active, be part of a team, make quality friends, be a friend, and much, much more. We are so blessed to be able to live in this world and do the things we do—yet while reading Mark Cahill's book, *The One Thing You Can't Do in Heaven*, I have been reminded that I sometimes miss out on the most important thing that we're to do while here on earth, and that is to share our faith with others. The dreaded "E" word—evangelism. Many will say, "That is the pastor's job" or "I don't know what to say" or "They won't listen to me." Those may all be true statements, but it doesn't get us out of our responsibility as followers of Christ. One compelling statement Cahill makes in his book is, "Friends don't let friends go to hell." If we truly care about the ones we love, won't we naturally want to tell them about the most important thing in our life?

What I am realizing from day to day is that the things of this earth really don't mean a whole lot. Winning games, having new cars or the latest fashion trends—all of these are nice, but not one of them comes close to what we have in store for us someday with Christ. I'm not encouraging you to forget everything you have in this life, but don't forsake and forget about the *One* who gave life to you. One young man in Cahill's book said that he wanted to be a Christian but still be cool. Cahill replied that going to heaven someday *would* be cool. Cahill went on to tell him that what would really be cool was if he told others about Jesus—the most important thing in life—and his friends went to heaven with him. With that, the young man acknowledged the truth in Cahill's words.

Today, cherish the important things in your life, but don't forget to live out the most important thing—serving Christ!

GO:

1. What are the most important things in your life?

2. How important is following Jesus to you as compared to other things?

3. Today, how can you start to share your faith with others?

WORKOUT:

Matthew 28:18–20
Mark 12:30
Philippians 3:12–15

Snowflakes

"I praise you because I am fearfully and wonderfully made; your works are wonderful, I know that full well" (Psalm 139:14 NIV).

SET:

Athletes are like snowflakes. Let me explain. They come in all shapes and sizes. Many are similar in their traits and looks, but no two athletes are the same—just like snowflakes. That is what makes them so unique. Each have their qualities that, when combined with a group, can make a difference in the outcome of an event.

Do you know that God made you like a snowflake? I know, you're thinking, *Did he just call me a flake?* Well, if the shoe fits... No, seriously—God made you like no other. Even twins that look identical on the outside have something that makes them different. The psalmist writes, "I am fearfully and wonderfully made...." People sometimes have a problem with not being like someone else. We all know people we long to be like or wish for some of their abilities or traits, but we need to be content with who God made us to be. He loves us just as we are and wants us to be more like Him each day.

So as far as I can tell, it's cool to be a flake...a snowflake for Christ! Be different; be unique for Him and His glory. You have the abilities that God has given you so you'll use them for Him. Who cares if you can't dunk or hit a ball 500 feet? You have something God has given you that He has given no one else... that is simply being *you* and who He created *you* to be.

Use your abilities and gifts with others to make something special for Christ!

GO:

1. How caught up are you in trying to be someone you're not?

2. Is it difficult for you to accept who God has made you to be? Why?

3. Today, how can you be a "snowflake" for Christ, uniquely different for *Him*?

WORKOUT:

Genesis 1:27
Isaiah 43:1
Ephesians 2:10

Get in the Race

READY:

"I have hidden your word in my heart that I might not sin against you" (Psalm 119:11 NIV).

SET:

It was the first race of his freshman year in high school in his small Indiana town. Was he ready? Had he trained properly? Who was the competition? These thoughts rushed through his head as he entered the starting blocks of the 400-meter relay.

Timing, precision, and teamwork were all a part of this outstanding race. Was he worthy to be on this team as a freshman and then have the extra responsibility to lead off? He had had a great junior high career, setting eight school records, but this was high school, the big time!

Feet set in the blocks...inside lane...judges ready... Teammates anxiously awaited their turn to run. Runners to your mark...set... *bang!* The young freshman dashed ahead, blazing down the track. He could hear everyone yelling his name. He was thinking he must be doing well. He looked up and saw his teammate jumping up and down with excitement as he approached the crucial point in the race, the first handoff.

Just then he realized...all the screams and excitement were not because he had arrived first at the handoff, but because he left his baton in the starting blocks. He was so excited about his first race in high school that he'd left without the proper equipment, the one thing he needed for this important race. Embarrassed and empty inside, he walked off the

140

track. He finished his day of events, but he never again forgot to start off the race right. He never again left his baton at the start. If we don't do what Psalm 119 says, we'll be like the freshman who left his baton in the blocks. We need God's Word each day to start off our daily race in the right way. But it does not end there. We need to daily hand off our baton (God's Word) to others, too. We need to share the goodness and grace of our loving Savior to each person we meet.

In the end, the young freshman grew up to have a great high school track career and set several records along the way—but one thing I never forgot was to carry my baton with me. Yes, that was my story. But now each day as I serve FCA in the Chicagoland area, I am challenged to start my race in God's Word so I can be ready to pass it to those around me, that they in turn can continue our race—God's race to His kingdom! God bless you as you pass on your spiritual baton to those in need!

GO:

1. When and why have you felt unprepared in a situation?

2. How often do you leave home without the right equipment and preparation?

3. How often do you start your day by spending time with God and hiding His Word in your heart?

WORKOUT:

1 Timothy 4:8
1 Timothy 4:12–16
1 Peter 3:15

Commitment 101

"Commit your activities to the LORD and your plans will be achieved" (Proverbs 16:3 HCSB).

"Commitment" is a big buzz word in sports today. Coaches are asking for commitment, players want to be committed, and schools are looking for a four-year commitment. But the word "commitment" is also used very loosely these days. I personally believe we need more athletes who are committed to their academic success before their athletic careers, but I'm old-school on that one.

When it comes to commitment, Jesus Christ wants us to be committed as well. He desires our commitment. When did you last say, "Lord, I am committing this to You"? In the verse for today, we read that if we commit our work to the Lord, our plans will succeed. Now, that does not say we will win, but we will be successful. When we walk with the Lord, we are guaranteed ultimate victory with Him in the end.

Committing everything to the Lord is a moment-by-moment adventure, not just a one-and-done. Everything we do, everything we are, everything about us needs to be completely committed to Christ. Wow! You might say that sounds like a lot to ask, but it is the *only* way we can be totally committed to Christ. Anything less just doesn't add up. Are you struggling with commitment in life? If so, first commit all that you are to Christ and then go from there. Once you are fully committed to Him, things will work out in the end.

GO:

1. How committed are you? And to what?

2. What percentage would you rate your commitment to Christ?

3. Today, how can you start being committed to Christ with all that you are?

WORKOUT:

Psalm 37:4–6
1 Peter 4:19
Revelation 3:15–16

One Day Better Commitment

After reading the sports devotional book *One Day Better*, I have decided that I need to make the following changes/commitments to grow as an athlete and family member and in my life with Christ:

_____

_____

_____

_____

_____

_____

_____

_____

_____

_____

Signature

_____

Date

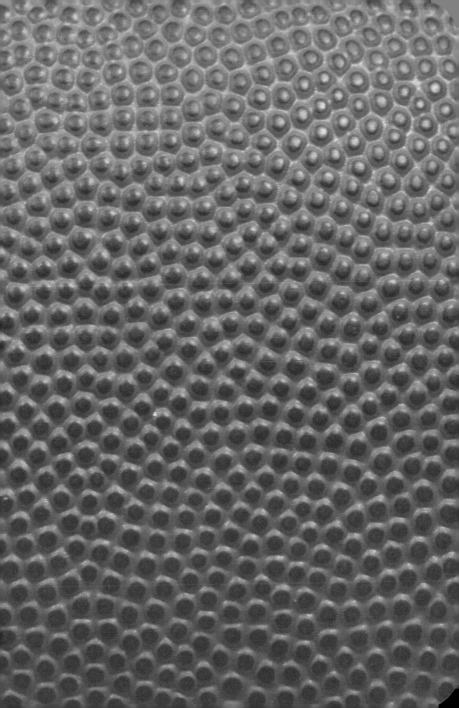